SEP 1 6 2010

D1270027

Japan in World History

DISCARDED

BRADFORD WG
PUBLIC LIBRARY

The
New
Oxford
World
History

Japan in World History

James L. Huffman

OXFORD

UNIVERSITY PRESS

2010

BRADFORD WG LIBRARY
100 HOLLAND COURT, BOX 130
BRADFORD, ONT. L3Z 2A7

OXFORD
UNIVERSITY PRESS

Oxford University Press, Inc., publishes works that further
Oxford University's objective of excellence
in research, scholarship, and education.

Oxford   New York
Auckland   Cape Town   Dar es Salaam   Hong Kong   Karachi
Kuala Lumpur   Madrid   Melbourne   Mexico City   Nairobi
New Delhi   Shanghai   Taipei   Toronto

With offices in
Argentina   Austria   Brazil   Chile   Czech Republic   France   Greece
Guatemala   Hungary   Italy   Japan   Poland   Portugal   Singapore
South Korea   Switzerland   Thailand   Turkey   Ukraine   Vietnam

Copyright © 2010 by James L. Huffman

Published by Oxford University Press, Inc.
198 Madison Avenue, New York, NY 10016

www.oup.com

Oxford is a registered trademark of Oxford University Press.

All rights reserved. No part of this publication may be reproduced,
stored in a retrieval system, or transmitted, in any form or by any means,
electronic, mechanical, photocopying, recording, or otherwise,
without the prior permission of Oxford University Press.

Library of Congress Cataloging-in-Publication Data
Huffman, James L.
Japan in world history / James L. Huffman.
p.   cm. — (New Oxford world history)
Includes bibliographical references and index.
ISBN 978-0-19-536809-3; ISBN 978-0-19-536808-6 (pbk.)
1. Japan—History.   2. Japan—Foreign relations.
3. World history.   I. Title.
DS835.H79 2010
952—dc22
2009019041

1 3 5 7 9 8 6 4 2

Printed in the United States of America
on acid-free paper

*Frontispiece: Japan's pioneer journalist Fukuchi Gen'ichirō,
a great lover of the latest Western attire, reports on the Satsuma
Rebellion in 1877.* Woodblock print by Kobayashi Kiyochika.
Courtesy of Mainichi Shimbunsha.

To my students, at Wittenberg and Dartmouth,
Who constantly challenged me to see history as a human thing

Contents

Editors' Preface

This book is part of the New Oxford World History, an innovative series that offers readers an informed, lively, and up-to-date history of the world and its people that represents a significant change from the "old" world history. Only a few years ago, world history generally amounted to a history of the West—Europe and the United States—with small amounts of information from the rest of the world. Some versions of the "old" world history drew attention to every part of the world *except* Europe and the United States. Readers of that kind of world history could get the impression that somehow the rest of the world was made up of exotic people who had strange customs and spoke difficult languages. Still another kind of "old" world history presented the story of areas or peoples of the world by focusing primarily on the achievements of great civilizations. One learned of great buildings, influential world religions, and mighty rulers but little of ordinary people or more general economic and social patterns. Interactions among the world's peoples were often told from only one perspective.

This series tells world history differently. First, it is comprehensive, covering all countries and regions of the world and investigating the total human experience—even those of so-called peoples without histories living far from the great civilizations. "New" world historians thus share in common an interest in all of human history, even going back millions of years before there were written human records. A few "new" world histories even extend their focus to the entire universe, a "big history" perspective that dramatically shifts the beginning of the story back to the Big Bang. Some see the "new" global framework of world history today as viewing the world from the vantage point of the moon, as one scholar put it. We agree. But we also want to take a close-up view, analyzing and reconstructing the significant experiences of all of humanity.

This is not to say that everything that has happened everywhere and in all time periods can be recovered or is worth knowing, but that there is much to be gained by considering both the separate and interrelated stories of different societies and cultures. Making these connections is still another crucial ingredient of the "new" world history. It emphasizes connectedness and interactions of all kinds—cultural, economic, political, religious, and social—involving peoples, places, and processes. It makes comparisons and finds similarities. Emphasizing both the comparisons and interactions is critical to developing a global framework that can deepen and broaden historical understanding, whether the focus is on a specific country or region or on the whole world.

The rise of the new world history as a discipline comes at an opportune time. The interest in world history in schools and among the general public is vast. We travel to one another's nations, converse and work with people around the world, and are changed by global events. War and peace affect populations worldwide as do economic conditions and the state of our environment, communications, and health and medicine. The New Oxford World History presents local histories in a global context and gives an overview of world events seen through the eyes of ordinary people. This combination of the local and the global further defines the new world history. Understanding the workings of global and local conditions in the past gives us tools for examining our own world and for envisioning the interconnected future that is in the making.

Bonnie G. Smith

Anand Yang

Preface

The sweeping survey is regarded as one of the most objective types of historical writing; in truth, even that form reflects the biases and ideologies of its writer. As the influential British historian Edward Hallett Carr told us, "It used to be said that facts speak for themselves. This is, of course untrue. The facts speak only when the historian calls on them."[1]

Born on a Midwestern farm not long before the Japanese bombed Pearl Harbor, I approach Japan's past as an outsider, albeit a sympathetic one. Japan is, after all, Asian; I am American. Since the early 1900s, Japan has been highly urban; I grew up rural. Japan is Shintō, Buddhist, and secular; I am Christian. But while my experiences render me an outsider, they also have given me a deep affection for the country. The exhilaration I felt when, with my wife Judith, I first encountered Japan—the smell of *tatami*-mat flooring in our apartment, the gentle aromas of the garden beyond the veranda, the pulse of Tokyo trains, the majesty of Mount Fuji, sitting there among wisps of clouds, the challenge of Buddhist ideas about impermanence and nonattachment, the humanity of our neighbors—has never left me. Those early months warned me against equating difference with inferiority, even as they schooled me in the exhilaration of seeing things in fresh ways. I hope these pages will do the same for readers.

My early years also affected my understanding of politics and economics. I spent most of the 1960s in college, too much influenced by my upbringing to imbibe the decade's free-living culture but deeply in tune with my fellow students' naive view that we could revolutionize the world. I drove to downtown Minneapolis as a reporter one steaming summer night in the midsixties and took notes while angry blacks and whites confronted each other. I skipped class in Tokyo to demonstrate against the war in Vietnam. Those experiences have given me an abiding sympathy for people who challenge established regimes in the name of justice. They also have made me aware of how imperfectly human people are, on each side of every issue.

And the hours spent on my childhood farm hoeing strawberry plants under a searing August sun, or feeding turkeys on freezing November mornings, have convinced me that history consists of more than the ideas and activities of leaders. When historians ignore commoners, when they leave out women, farmers, workers, and outcasts, they muffle important voices. Almost as serious, they give us an inadequate—thus inaccurate—picture of human development. If my highly traditional training leads me to acknowledge the central role of elite institutions in propelling change, my hours selling muskmelons at the local market compel me to pay attention to average women and men—and to feel a certain guilt for telling their story less than adequately.

Historians long have talked, quite sensibly, about several themes in Japanese history: the role of the long-unbroken imperial line; the many centuries of peace; the lasting impact of warrior values following the samurai-dominated medieval era; the importance of Buddhism; the subordination of the individual to the group. Those themes will appear in this book, but there will also be others—no less important for having been noted less frequently. Japan's location, less than a hundred miles from Asia's continental coast, is one important theme. Like Great Britain off Europe, Japan has defined itself and interacted with other countries in ways explainable only by the happenstance of geography. The novelist Endō Shūsaku called his homeland a cul-de-sac and a "mud swamp,"[2] a place where foreign movements and ideas came and then simply stayed put, neither leaving nor maturing in normal ways. His point of reference was Christianity, but he could just as well have been describing the Chinese writing system, modulated and distorted to fit spoken Japanese; or Chan Buddhism, reborn in Zen aesthetics; or Western cartoons, which evolved into *anime*. From earliest times, Japan has alternately interacted with foreigners and excluded them—often in extreme ways that would have been unlikely for a continental nation. The pattern took many forms across the centuries, but the one that cries out most sharply for explanation came in the modern era when Japan first shut itself off from most Western influences, then interacted intensely after the mid-1800s, then followed separatist, expansive inclinations into World War II—only to reengage the world as an economic power after the 1950s.

Closely related has been Japan's complex relationship with the rest of Asia, particularly with China. Even before history, the Japanese knew about China's advanced bronzes and political sophistication, yet they remained almost obstinately illiterate and quite isolated, though relatively prosperous. In certain periods, the Japanese treated Chinese systems and philosophies with great respect; in the 1400s they even accepted tribute status with China. Yet in most eras they held the Middle Kingdom at arm's length, adapting Chinese forms (for example, the governmental structure) but not their heart (China's civil service exam system). After China failed to modernize in the 1800s, the Japanese treated it with undisguised contempt, typically calling it Shina (China) rather than the traditional, respectful Chūgoku (Middle Kingdom). When the nineteenth-century scholar Fukuzawa Yukichi suggested that Japan should "cast Asia off,"[3] he was drawing on a long tradition of skepticism and ambivalence about Japan's relationship with the continent, a tradition that still plagues interactions with China today.

A theme of a different kind is Japan's ability to thrive against remarkable odds. The archipelago is small, and mountains cover four-fifths of what land space there is, crowding its residents together in densely packed communities. The islands also lack natural resources. And they have been wracked continuously by earthquakes, typhoons, and volcanic eruptions. Yet from earliest times, the Japanese have used these very impediments to produce the richest of material and artistic cultures. They crafted humankind's earliest ceramics and wrote its first novel; they turned out unique poetic forms, flowerless gardens, artwork that glorified the primitive and relished the imperfect. Confronted by China's superiority in the seventh century, they undertook reforms that brought them abreast of that land by the eighth. Frightened by Western imperialists in the 1850s, they transformed themselves into a world power by the early 1900s. Asking how they achieved so much with so little is one of the historian's most daunting tasks.

So is the search for explanations of the country's ability to thrive despite an endless succession of allegedly ineffective political regimes. When two leading historians described the 1700s and 1800s as a "long but losing battle for the political authorities,"[4] they could have been speaking of any era. The 700s, when the capital was located in Nara, saw bloody, uninterrupted struggles over power; the Heian era, which followed, witnessed some of history's most inefficient administrations; during the medieval era, no group ruled competently. Genuinely effective administrations have appeared only rarely. Yet in almost every period, the economy has thrived; inventions have abounded; peasants have grown better off; religious movements have spread; and commoners, elites, and businessmen have produced the vibrant culture I have already alluded to. Even the late 1400s, when the country had no central authority worth the name, gave rise to impressive economic growth and some of history's most original arts. Where did the growth-genius come from? This book will attempt to provide some clues.

A final characteristic of Japan's past is the often overlooked dynamism of commoner culture. Scholars typically praise the cultural brilliance of the early Nara years yet ignore the heavy influence that songs, tales, and religious enthusiasms from the countryside had on that culture. When the modernizers began writing a constitution in the 1880s, mountain villagers composed their own drafts, but the elites paid little attention. When the farmers took up arms against high taxes and corrupt officials, officials paid much more attention but still gave the commoners no respect. Even plebeian arts—the woodblock prints of the Tokugawa merchants, the rock music of late twentieth-century bands—have provoked uncomprehending condescension more often than respect from the arbiters of culture. But in every era, what the historian Irokawa Daikichi calls the "common people's vitality and recalcitrance"[5] has fueled much of society's innovation and growth. Those people's stories may well be the most interesting; their experiences particularly need to be told.

James L. Huffman

Note: Personal names in this work follow the traditional Japanese order, with the surname preceding the given name, unless the reverse order was used in the original.

Japan in
World History

Before the Brush
(to 645 CE)

Long before history, said the ancients, the sun goddess, Amaterasu, ruled over Japan, bringing light, warmth, and fertility. Under her guidance, the natural patterns continued—spring, summer, fall, and winter—all in their order. Then, Amaterasu's brother Susanoo, the ill-tempered god of storms and the underworld, caused trouble, demolishing the ridges between rice fields in the spring and letting spotted colts loose, to lie down on the ripened rice, in autumn. Dismayed, she protested by shutting herself in a mountain cave and plunging the earth into darkness. Now it was the other deities who became distressed. In the words of one of the earliest chronicles, their cries "were everywhere abundant, like summer flies; and all manner of calamities arose," until someone hit on the idea of staging a festival outside the cave, to tempt her with loud merrymaking. When the goddess peeked out to see what all the noise was about, they pulled her from the cave, sealed the entrance, and assured the return of light.[1]

Thus runs one of the mythological explanations of Japan in ancient times. The scientific story is duller—and more reliable. In the geographers' account, Japan (called Nihon by the Japanese themselves) is an archipelago of four major islands and 7,000 smaller ones off the eastern shore of the Eurasian land mass. It has a small land area, covering just 145,000 square miles, which could fit into the United States twenty-five times over. Its population, on the other hand, is huge: roughly 127 million, or more than 40 percent of the U.S. population in the early twenty-first century. Largely without natural resources, it is forced to rely on imports from around the world to run its industrial plants.

If the scientific facts are more reliable, the legends are probably more insightful, for they give us a glimpse of the country's soul, a suggestion of what mattered to people as the stories evolved. Amaterasu's cave escapade, for example, illustrates the profound way people's lives and the natural patterns have been shaped by mountains. Steep slopes make up three-fourths of the country's land area, and those slopes sit atop four tectonic plates, which have shifted and

Gyōbō Iwaya Cave in the Takachiho region of eastern Kyushu, near where the sun goddess, Amaterasu, reputedly hid herself in a cave to protest the storm god's reckless pranks; the myths say 800 deities gathered here to devise a strategy for getting her to come out. Photo by Jeremy Hunter.

collided across the millennia, forming lush green peaks and valleys even as they have produced horrific earthquakes and volcanic eruptions. The mountains also have forced almost all the people onto a few major plains, where they live crowded together in some of the world's most densely populated spaces. And the storm god's deviltry speaks of the temperate-zone seasonal patterns that have for so long dominated Japan's annual cycle of planting and harvesting, worshiping and celebrating. When an enthusiastic newspaper correspondent wrote generations ago about "glorious cherry—the queen of flowers...the beautiful emblem of the true sons of the Yamato's land,"[2] he was heralding a seasonal blossom-viewing ritual that had inspired people since the Japanese began calling their land Yamato more than 1,500 years ago.

Another of the prehistoric tales—that of a queen sailing off to conquer Korea—illustrates the impact that location has had on Japan's historical development. According to the *Kojiki* (Record of ancient matters), the empress Jingū one day received divine instruction that "there is a land to the west," filled with "gold and silver, as well as all sorts of eye-dazzling precious treasures," that was hers for the taking. When her skeptical husband said he saw "only the ocean" to the west, he was struck dead, and it fell to Jingū to subdue Korea.[3] Few historians believe the tale, but no one questions the importance of one of its key themes: that Japan's location just off the coast of continental Asia would have a monumental influence on the country's history. In prehistoric times, the islands were connected to Asia by land bridges, but for the last 18,000 years or so they have lain 130 miles off the continent. That has placed Japan close enough to its Asian neighbors to allow for rich cultural interchange yet far enough away to keep it independent, a fact that has given foreign relations a unique character: sometimes constructive, sometimes destructive, sometimes unusual, but always dynamic and interesting.

Another of the timeless ancient myths describes Izanagi, a creator of the Japanese islands, returning from a visit to the underworld covered with filth. "I have been to a most unpleasant land, a horrible, unclean land," he complained. "Therefore I shall purify myself." So saying, he "dived into the middle stream and bathed," giving birth to a new deity with each movement and demonstrating yet one more thing that has made Japan what it is: water.[4] Down the mountain slopes every spring rush hundreds of rivers that irrigate the fields and power the hydroelectric plants. Around the country's 18,500 miles of coastline surge the vast Pacific waters that provide endless varieties of fish for city markets and seaweed for evening tables. And from the clouds that blow in from the south every spring and summer fall the heavy rains that flood paddies and make Japan one of the world's biggest producers of rice. The country may not have much gas, oil, iron, or coal, but it compensates through the use of water.

If Japan's natural setting has produced a vibrant culture, however, it has frustrated those who want detailed information about the past, as the land's early millennia are shrouded in mystery. For reasons that never have been satisfactorily explained—but which sprang at least partly from the archipelago's isolation from the continent—writing came late to Japan. Not until at least the fourth century CE, tens of thousands of years after people began inhabiting the islands, did they take up the brush and begin to communicate on paper, and even then they used Chinese characters, or *kanji*, to transcribe their own spoken language. As a result, we are left with nothing but archaeological artifacts, myths, and spotty foreign observations to tell us what happened well into what we call the "common" era.

Traditionally, historians have divided Japan's early centuries into three eras. The Jōmon period, dating as far back as 16,500 years ago, lasted until the fourth century BCE, and was named for the sophisticated *jōmon* (rope-marked) pottery produced by a society of hunters and gatherers. The culture that followed, named Yayoi—for the place in Tokyo where many of its artifacts have been found—saw the emergence of wet-rice agriculture, iron and bronze implements, and the country's first towns; it existed roughly from 300 BCE to 300 CE. The third period, Kofun, is named for its large earthen mound-tombs, many of them huge, which preserved the holdings of a rising ruling class between the fourth and seventh centuries. In recent years, scholars have tended to explain Japan's early emergence less in terms of the rigid Jōmon-Yayoi-Kofun labels, however, and more as a gradual evolution, with occasional sharp curves, from the preagricultural epoch through the rise of agriculture and finally the development of a state.

People have inhabited Japan for at least 35,000 years, but we know more about its geology than its inhabitants before 10,000 BCE. Across most of the millennia, the human population apparently rose and fell with fluctuations in global temperatures. By the peak of the last great cold or glacial era 18,000 years ago, Japan probably supported no more than a few hundred people living in caves or on mountainsides and hunting free-roaming animals. A period of global warming then set in, and the population began to grow—and change. By about 6,000 BCE (the early Jōmon period), temperatures had surpassed those we now consider normal, and as a result the oceans rose to perhaps eighteen feet above today's levels, shrinking the islands' land mass and precipitating Japan's first significant advance in civilization, as people were forced to live closer to each other. Animals were driven into mountain valleys, making them easier to hunt. The people—who were shorter than the mainlanders, with men averaging a little over five feet and women just under—began building shelters for protection; some constructed dugout canoes and began traveling far out to sea, to fish with harpoons and hooks. They also began trading stone implements, which now were being made in significant numbers, and there is evidence that exchanges with people on the Asian continent became fairly common. Archaeological discoveries also suggest the growth of religious ceremonies in these early Jōmon years, many of them connected with fertility or with appeasing the spirits of the dead, and they reveal people eating more and more plants and nuts.

To the very end, Jōmon remained largely preagricultural, with food provided by hunting, fishing, and foraging, but its inhabitants showed increasing sophistication in the ways they put their lives together. The era's most distinctive development lay in the production of what many archaeologists consider to be humankind's earliest pottery, with artifacts dating from as early as 14,500 BCE.[5] Although clay figurines were made earlier in Europe, there is no evidence of ceramic vases anywhere else at this early date. Equally impressive was the creative nature of the pottery, much of which generally is thought to have been crafted by women, as it was in other ancient societies. Archaeologists have found more than 250 different types of vessels across the archipelago, decorated with rope impressions, rouletting, clay appliqué, and marks made by pressing fingers, nails, or shells against the clay. The pots were used for a variety of functions: boiling seaweed, steaming vegetables, serving and storing food, holding plants, and decorating. Their makers, in other words, were both skilled and innovative, their functions both utilitarian and artistic.

The Jōmon pottery reveals a gradual but distinct improvement in the quality and organization of life on the islands. By perhaps 5,000 BCE, many communities were staying put, living in a single location throughout the year, collecting emergent plants in the spring, gathering nuts in the fall, and fishing and hunting all year long. They also were using the rope-marked pots to evaporate ocean water and produce salt, which would preserve the produce they gathered over the summer. As the era advanced, they began living in constructed houses, most often pit dwellings with low walls and thatched roofs that maintained a fairly

This clay pot, from the third millennium BCE, illustrates the rope markings and elaborate designs typical of the Jōmon era. TNM Image Archives.

constant temperature year-round. Communities of anywhere from 30 to 200 households congregated in some regions, disposing of their wastes in shell mounds on the edges of the settlements; in one northern Honshu site, archaeologists have found more than 600 dwellings, though it is not clear that all were in use at the same time. These relatively safer, more settled conditions also fueled an increase in the population, which may have reached a quarter of a million by about 3,000 BCE, before it dipped again during another global cooling in the late Jōmon years.

By about 1,000 BCE, a shared, country-wide culture had begun to emerge. That does not mean that there were no regional differences. Indeed, peoples in different areas are known to have developed their own specialties by then, with the northern Umataka people making talc and jade jewelry, and the people of central Japan creating pots and figurines bedecked with fertile, auspicious animal symbols. Alongside the variations, however, came increasing similarities in pottery and implement styles that revealed regional intermingling. When the earliest chronicles said the first emperor was "enabled to establish the world in peace" by shaping the "clay of the Heavenly Mount Kagu" into eighty platters of sacred clay and then sacrificing "to all the Gods,"[6] they were transmitting myths rather than history, but they also were describing a spreading cultural connectedness.

The most puzzling of the shared characteristics is a negative: the absence, even late in Jōmon, of key elements that characterized life in Japan's advanced Asian neighbor, China. Indeed, one of the most enduring questions about Japan's prehistoric past is why a land that had produced the world's first ceramic vessels, a country that had imported continental foodstuffs such as yams, taro, and millet, failed for more than a thousand years to emulate two of early China's most striking features: the development of a sophisticated writing system and the production of bronze vessels. What is clear is that the effects of being situated off the fringe of the continent were powerful, even at this early stage. Separated from the rest of Asia by treacherous seas, the Japanese would find it easy to adopt certain continental offerings while ignoring others.

During the transitional time between the Jōmon and Yayoi periods, the continental influence became much stronger. Indeed, the relatively quick appearance after 300 BCE of iron implements and wheel-formed pottery, along with the rise of the archipelago's first regional centers, once led scholars to speculate that Japan might have been invaded. Today, historians and archaeologists generally have a different opinion. From a combination of artifacts and reports by Chinese officials, they have concluded that Japan now experienced an upsurge of immigrants from Korea, where wars and political struggles were forcing people from their homes. These newcomers introduced continental practices and technologies that the people of northern Kyushu then adapted and spread throughout the islands.

Wet-rice farming was at the heart of the new culture. Rudimentary agricultural practices had begun in earlier centuries—after an ancient god produced rice from her belly and "sowed...the rice seed in the narrow fields and in the long fields of Heaven," according to one legend[7]—but it was not until the Yayoi years that planting and harvesting became the primary means of securing food. Archaeological surveys of more than a hundred Yayoi-era paddies show a revolutionary change in the way rice was produced, as villagers started using the farming techniques of the immigrants from the continent, along with their iron and bronze implements. They began to open new fields (often in wet swamps), to plant the short-grain rice seeds used in Korea, and to dig ditches that would bring water to dry paddies. They also began to domesticate pigs for meat, even as they continued to hunt wild animals and gather herbs, nuts, and mountain plants. And they worked the fields with new implements made of wood, stone, and iron: axes, hoes, rakes, and mallets. They also began constructing wooden storage bins, placing them on stilts to keep grains drier in humid areas.

Agriculture changed island life dramatically. More people began to live in villages, and they built bigger houses. They dug wells to maintain the water supply and wove textiles to make clothing. They made pottery on a turntable, allowing workmen to produce utilitarian dishes and

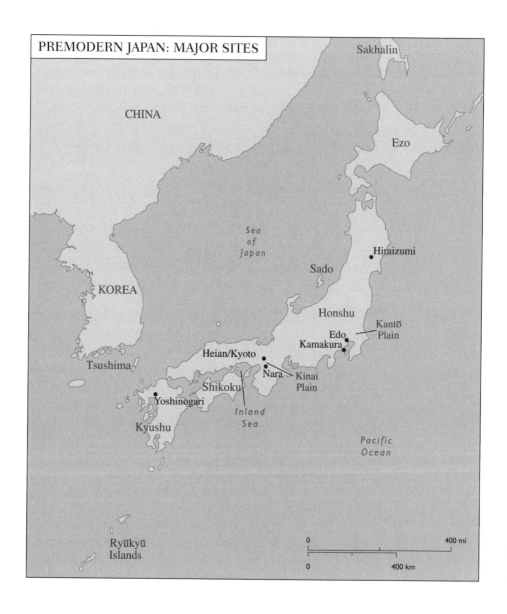

PREMODERN JAPAN: MAJOR SITES

cups in greater numbers. Trade flourished along the coast too, even as society grew more stratified and regional centers emerged to dominate the affairs of scattered hamlets. And many of the elements of Shintō, Japan's indigenous religion, took root: the belief that each mountain, river, or rock had a god-spirit or *kami*; the appeal to shamans and rites to appease those spirits; the celebration of sex and fertility; and the use of water to purge pollution.

Excavations of one of Japan's first significant towns, Yoshinogari in northern Kyushu, provide concrete illustration of how dramatically life had changed by the middle Yayoi years. The digs there, carried out in the late 1980s, show a lively commercial life, with the residents of more than 350 dwellings engaged in a range of jobs, from weaving and bead-making to the casting of bronzes. They also indicate class differences, with commoners and officials inhabiting separate areas, separated by a moat. Large storehouses, thought to have housed tax grains collected from surrounding villages, suggest the region's growing political sophistication, as those in the central town came to dominate surrounding hamlets, while headless skeletons and arrow-pierced bones in the commoners' graves give evidence of the battles that made Yoshi-nogari dominant. It also seems clear, from the scores of glass beads and the Korean-style dagger in the rulers' burial site, that the people of Yoshinogari were actively engaged in international trade.

Our most detailed knowledge of the Yayoi centuries comes from Japan's first written records, prepared not by the nonwriting Japanese, but by Chinese observers of what they called the land of Wa, a fertile place "warm and mild" enough for people to "live on raw vegetables and go about barefooted" even in winter.[8] At the end of their own dynastic histories, Chinese writers often appended brief reports on the "barbarian" countries, notes that bring Yayoi society to life in ways no accumulation of artifacts ever could. A simple visitor's comment, for example, that early-Yayoi leaders "from time to time send their trib-utes"[9] to Chinese rulers gives us a level of understanding about evolving relationships and Japan's own changing political structure that artifacts will never afford.

These records speak a good deal about Yayoi lifestyle and values. They show a law-abiding, hardworking people, probably living in northern Kyushu, who loved pleasure and valued creativity. According to the *History of the Kingdom of Wei*, the Japanese of the third century CE wore "pink and scarlet" makeup, ate with their fingers, drank liquor, lived for as long as a century, observed class distinctions, and treated men and women equally, though "men of importance" had as many as five wives and the higher classes kept slaves. The writer reports that "all men, old or young, are covered by tattoos" that are supposed to keep away malicious spirits when they go fishing. The men wore their hair down over their ears and often dressed in loincloths, while women wore "an unlined coverlet... by slipping the head through an opening in the center." Fishermen were "fond of diving into the water to get fish and shells," and when people made ocean voyages, they took along a "fortune keeper" who appeased the spirits by staying away from women and leaving his hair uncombed and his body unwashed. If the journey went well, he was given gifts, possibly even slaves; if it failed, he was killed.

Both the written records and the archeological evidence depict an organized, competitive society, with at least thirty power centers, which the Chinese called "countries," struggling for dominance by the early Common Era. The regional rulers insisted that commoners bow when "high-echelon men" passed. And they fought for supremacy. The Wei history describes "disturbances and warfare" that had been going on for many decades: a reference to the very move toward centralization that Yoshinogari's thirty-foot-deep moats, watch towers, and headless skeletons illustrate so vividly.

One characteristic that set Yayoi Japan apart from China was the prominence of women in powerful positions. The people of Wa did more than merely treat both genders equally; they chose women as leaders. The first important person referred to by name in the Wei—or any—record is Himiko,[10] an unmarried woman in a place known as Yamatai, who took the reins of state after decades of war and, as "Queen of Wa," presided over a pacified realm in the early third century. The Wei account says that she had the ability to divine spirits, was assisted by a younger brother, and had "one thousand maidservants, but... only one manservant." When violence flared under a male successor, officials turned to another female, Himiko's teenaged relative Iyo, who restored order again. Though the location and specifics of Himiko's rule remain unclear, historians regard her as one of a number of local chieftains who fought for control of ever-expanding territories. Some scholars suggest that the fighting might have been triggered partly by climate warming in the Yayoi era, which raised sea levels, flooded agricultural areas, and caused competition for land.[11]

These Chinese accounts also describe a people keenly aware of the power and sophistication of Korea and China. They make it clear that the Japanese kingdoms had long been sending representatives to the continent. Himiko, the Wei history says, sent three tribute missions to the Chinese emperors, giving them slaves and cloth. Iyo sent thirty slaves and 5,000 "white gems," in addition to many pieces of carved jade and twenty bolts of brocade cloth. And the Chinese emperors responded with gifts of their own, including scores of bronze mirrors and warrants certifying the gift-givers' rights to reign in their own regions.

Japan by the fourth century CE, while far from unified, was thus taking on the appearances of a country, replete with settled communities, market towns, local leaders fighting for control, and formal interchanges between regional overlords and foreign officials—what today we would call diplomacy. Moreover, the appearance at this time of great mound-tombs suggests that the political order was moving toward something more substantial and more permanent. Called *kofun* ("old mounds"), these tombs gave evidence to the rise of a rich ruling class and lent their name to an epochal period, from about 300 to the mid-600s CE, when Japan developed a centralized state structure and moved from the foggy mists of prehistory to the greater clarity of records-based history. A few burial mound sites already had been constructed in the middle Yayoi years, one of the first being the fifteen-foot-high, 130-foot-long mound in Yoshinogari. But it was at the end of Yayoi that they proliferated, showing up by the tens of thousands, primarily in the Nara region of central Honshu. Many of these tombs were huge—some of them as long as 1,500 feet—and more than 5,000 of them were shaped like keyholes, surrounded by up to three moats. On the inside, they contained objects that had been important in the lives of the deceased, particularly bronze mirrors and jewelry. On the outside, they were surrounded by as many as 20,000 clay figurines, called *haniwa*, that represented nearly every aspect of Japanese life and society: scholars, houses, peasants wearing earrings, horses, nobles, dancers, tattooed men, musical instruments, animals. Some think the *haniwa* were used to keep the mounds from eroding, others that they were meant to protect the departed from malingering spirits—but all agree that they demonstrated quite vividly the wealth of the emerging ruling class and the impact of continental culture.

Japan's move now toward a centralized system was propelled in significant ways by events on the continent. The third through sixth centuries marked a time of incessant warfare in China and Korea, and the battles forced new waves of uprooted families, particularly from Korea, to come to Japan, where they intermingled with local populations. They brought with them irrigation technologies and a writing system; they provided expertise for building temples and pottery kilns; they demonstrated accounting techniques and suggested new administrative

Clay figurines (haniwa) *such as this young maiden surrounded the mound tombs of powerful figures in the Kofun era of the fourth to seventh centuries. Though the precise purpose of* haniwa *remains unclear, they tell us much about life in the era before writing: that women wore dresses and hats, that horses were used in battle, and that men sometimes wore tattoos.* TNM Image Archives.

structures, as well as new dyeing and weaving methods. The immigrants also brought saddles and bridles, facilitating the use of horses in Japan's regional wars. Some scholars propose that the Korean immigrants actually took over the Japanese power structure in these years, but most think they were simply assimilated, teaching new skills and assisting in local power struggles.

Whatever the situation, the immigrants touched almost every area of Kofun-era life. Japan's population grew from well under a million in the late Jōmon cold period to an estimated five million by the end of the warmer Kofun years. And people lived better. While coastal hamlets suffered sometimes from pirates' incursions, most villagers had better incomes, better rice strains, and better protection against nature's whims, thanks to the new agricultural practices. A new clay cooking stove, called a *kamado*, made interiors less smoky and saved fuel. Religion became more complex now as the animistic practices of Shintō were challenged by the more organized, scripturally based doctrines of continental Buddhism. Within the ruling classes, new social relationships also emerged, as rulers designated prominent clans, called *uji*, to serve the court and assist with administration. The *uji* in turn controlled lesser families, called *be*, which were given specific tasks such as providing religious services, making saddles, serving as scribes, or running the kitchens of the powerful. These groups provided a basis for much of the social structure that would dominate status relationships for many centuries.

As society grew more uniform, a king-centered central state began to take shape. The story of its creation is told most interestingly, though hardly accurately, in Japan's earliest extant writings, the eighth-century *Kojiki* (Record of ancient matters) and *Nihon shoki* (Chronicle of Japan). Intended to justify the legitimacy of the emerging line of chieftains—often referred to as the sun line, because of their reputed origin in the sun goddess, Amaterasu—these works relate as fact Japan's most fundamental myths. They describe the divine origins of the land, in which the gods Izanagi and Izanami gave birth to each island, one after another. They narrate the descent of Amaterasu's grandson, Ninigi no Mikoto, from heaven to bring order to the islands. And in a tale that would shape Japan's self-identity in later centuries, they tell how the first emperor, Jimmu, journeyed to the Kinai plain of central Honshu—a "fair land encircled on all sides by blue mountains" at "the centre of the world"—to begin "the Heavenly task" of imperial rule.[12] Many of these tales drone on with mind-numbing lists of rulers and gods; others exude energy and fantasy. All of them, however, bespeak an effort by emergent families in the Kinai region to force diverse local and regional traditions into an overarching central story.

The more factual record of the emergence of the Yamato clan from Kinai as sovereigns during the Kofun years, which was put together by historians using a combination of artifacts, Chinese records, and the *Nihon shoki*, may lack the supernatural elements, but it is almost as interesting. Now the struggles among regional rivals continued even more intensely, with families from the Kinai region gaining preeminence by the 500s. In the early fourth century, Kinai lords such as Ōjin and Nintoku appear to have fought battles as far away as northern Kyushu and Korea. They also sought legitimacy from the continent, both by adopting Chinese rule patterns and by securing written approbation from the Chinese rulers. The chronicles tell us that Nintoku, for example, carefully observed the Confucian precept that officials must look out for the welfare of their subjects. Climbing a tower and seeing that "no smoke arose in the land," he concluded that "the people are poor, and...in the houses there are none cooking their rice," and then declared a three-year moratorium on farmers' labor taxes even though his own palace was crumbling.[13] The chronicles give a different description of the late fifth-century leader Yūryaku, who failed in his ambitious efforts to conquer southern and eastern Korea. They say "the Empire censured him, and called him 'The greatly wicked Emperor,' "[14] because he killed potential rivals so often and so wantonly.

The triumph of the Kinai rulers in the 500s and 600s as overlords of much of central and southern Japan (though not of the entire archipelago) was propelled, once more, by an interplay of continental and domestic elements. At home, the vicious struggles among regional rivals were balanced by the frequent construction of alliances, with relationships often cemented by marriages between powerful families. The foreign impact on this process showed up partly in the tactical military advantage that resulted from the use of imported horses and partly in the contributions of immigrant Korean craftsmen, scribes, and administrators to the building of the Kinai state, which by the mid-600s was centered in the gentle hills of Asuka, south of present-day Nara.

Equally important to the process was the foreigners' introduction of Buddhism. According to a *Nihon shoki* account, a Korean ruler sent the Asuka officials several scriptures and a statue of Buddha in the 550s—and in so doing, set off another power struggle. Two influential clans that had supervised the Yamato court's religious ceremonies, the Nakatomi and Mononobe, opposed the continental religion as foreign, while the rising Soga family espoused it. The intensity of their rivalry is apparent in an oft-told tale that had the Soga placing the Buddha statue in their home, only to have it thrown into a canal by worried officials when a pestilence hit the area. The struggle actually had more to do with political ambitions than with religious ideas or superstitious fears, however, and when Buddhism eventually triumphed, it left its mark on almost every facet of national life. It also propelled the Soga to political dominance.

Another woman leader, Suiko, was on the throne at the beginning of the seventh century, when Yamato kingship became firmly established. The daughter of a Soga mother, she ascended the throne in 593, after her half-brother, King Sushun, was assassinated, and for three decades she and her nephew/advisor Shōtoku Taishi acted as co-rulers, establishing Asuka as the center of Kinai power and instigating reforms that would clinch imperial control. Suiko's thirty-six years in office marked the longest imperial reign from her time until Mutsuhito became the Meiji emperor in 1868.

Shōtoku is more famous than his aunt, partly because the *Nihon shoki* made him into a saint: an infant who spoke at birth, a benefactor who, seeing a starving man beside the road, "gave him to eat and to drink and taking off his own raiment, clothed with it the starving man," a ruler whose death evoked cries that "heaven and earth have crumbled to ruin."[15] It is not clear, however, who merits credit for which of the reforms during their joint rule. What is certain is that the reforms were fundamental in consolidating the new king-dominated regime, and that they drew deep inspiration from China, which had been newly unified in the 580s under the Sui dynasty. Korea had become less important in the Japanese mind by now, having fallen under the shadow of its western neighbor. China, by contrast, had become a fountain of advanced civilization and administrative wisdom. As a result, the Asuka government attempted to consolidate rule by implementing Chinese administrative styles and emphasizing Confucian doctrines of loyalty, virtue, and harmony.

In more extensive fashion than ever before, the regime now sent sizeable missions to the continent, partly to engage in diplomatic relations and partly to learn more about China. One of the first of these missions, sent in 607, carried a charge from "the Son of Heaven in the land where the sun rises…to the Son of Heaven in the land where the sun sets," causing the Sui emperor to retort: "If memorials from barbarian states are written by persons who lack propriety, don't accept them."[16] The diplomatic niceties got worked out, and across the next two centuries a dozen official missions, sometimes numbering as many as 500 scholars, monks, craftsmen, and scribes, plied the dangerous waters between China and Japan. Some of the travelers stayed for more than a decade before returning home to share the knowledge they had gained. The fact that Japan over the next few generations constructed new land allocation systems, new law codes, new temples, and new capital cities—all based on the patterns of the Sui dynasty and its successor, the Tang—suggests how deeply the Japanese respected their Asian neighbor. It also suggests the self-confidence of Asuka rulers, for whom advanced knowledge abroad was seen as an opportunity rather than a threat.

Using the Chinese model, the Yamato state adopted a new cap-rank system, where status was accorded individually rather than by family, with rank indicated by the color of one's cap: purple for the highest ranks, followed by green, red, yellow, white, and black. It also compiled new law codes and produced the country's first official histories, though the manuscripts have since been lost. The most-quoted innovation was a seventeen-article statement of governing principles, issued in 604 and attributed to Shōtoku. Sometimes called Japan's first constitution, it actually was a set of ethical principles. "Harmony," began the first injunction, "is to be valued.... When those above are harmonious and those below are friendly, right views of things spontaneously gain acceptance." No student of Asia can read that without being struck by its Confucian tone. The same is true of articles that demanded "scrupulous" obedience to imperial commands, "decorous behavior," the avoidance of gluttony, and the selection of "wise men" as rulers. At the same time, several of the admonitions have a distinctly local flavor—the statement, for example, that the "lord is heaven," and the insistence that officials "attend the court early in the morning, and retire late," since "the whole day is hardly enough" to complete state work. The absence of Chinese concepts such as the necessity of ruling by "heaven's mandate" and recruiting officials through exams also demonstrates the independent mind with which the Yamato rulers applied Chinese models. A Chinese overlay added gravitas to the emergent court, but its foundations lay in the rolling Asuka countryside.[17]

The activity for which Shōtoku was best known was his espousal of Buddhism. While scholars argue about whether he kept his Soga relatives in check or smoothed their path to power, they agree that his espousal of that family's faith was crucial in turning Buddhism into Japan's most influential religion. He is credited not only with personal devotion but with writing seven commentaries that showed an impressive grasp of Indian Buddhist scriptures. He also advocated state support of the religion and had several temples built, including the Hōryūji, north of Asuka, which today holds one of Japan's foremost collections of Buddhist art. Temples across the Yamato region still honor Shōtoku as Japanese Buddhism's patron saint.

What of life in the countryside during these transitional generations? While the *Nihon shoki* slights the commoners, it does suggest that the villagers of Kyushu and central Honshu were coming to share both a similar culture and an image of themselves as part of a wider unit, something we today might call a state, even though a full half of the archipelago remained outside the Kinai rulers' control, and no one had yet used the word Nihon. Chinese visitors' records from this period describe a land in which status distinctions had become ubiquitous. Officials wore shoes "painted with lacquer, and tied on with strings," while the lower classes often went barefoot and were not allowed to wear jewelry. Commoners also were subjected to a relatively harsh legal system in which the king himself sometimes sat, cross-legged, as a judge, with punishments ranging from flogging to death. A suspect who denied guilt might be forced to pluck a snake from a jar, on the premise that "if he is guilty, his hand will be bitten." There were also heavy taxes to pay. Life was not all subservience, however; the Chinese accounts also describe celebrations on the first day of each month, marked by games, archery contests, and drinking. Villagers staged seasonal and religious festivals, too, and liked "chess, betting, juggling, and dice games."[18]

Following Shōtoku's death in 622 and that of Suiko in 628, conditions in the capital turned violent, as the Soga family made a grab for power. According to the early chronicles, the family constructed lavish homes, erected its own ancestral temple, built grand tombs, and even designated a Soga son to receive a cap designated for the king. In response, other ambitious families launched schemes of their own. The result was what the chronicles describe as one of the most dramatic political incidents in all of Japanese history: the murder of the head of the Soga family in front of Queen Kōgyoku while she was presiding over a ceremony in 645 to receive a diplomat from Korea. In the aftermath, various other Soga family members were killed, the Soga residences were destroyed, and the Nakatomi family was restored to the influence it had had before Buddhism came.

Though the accounts of the Soga overthrow may be embellished, there is no doubt that the episode presaged important changes in the style of Yamato administration, changes known by later generations as the *taika,* or "great reform." Laying the foundation from which Japan's *tennō* (emperor) system would develop, the rulers set about in the mid-600s to centralize taxes, create population registers, provide for court appointment of regional governors, and devise a system of state allocation of land to the people. They also created a produce tax to replace labor assessments and asserted that women had the right to remarry. Their basic goal was clear: to assert the total control of the Yamato ruler. As one of the reform edicts, reconstructed in the *Nihon shoki,* put it: "Now our hearts are one. There shall be one sovereign and ministers shall not oppose his rule. Should anyone break his oath, Heaven will send disasters and earth will send calamities....This is as clear as the sun and moon."[19]

Rival families and factions continued to vie for power over the next few decades, and the impact of the reforms was uneven, with the court's grip weakening as the distance from Kinai lengthened. Moreover, the northern third of Honshu island remained wholly outside the Yamato kingdom, inhabited by a trading, rice-growing, horse-raising people known derisively in the capital as Emishi or "toad barbarians."

Nonetheless, the early and middle 600s saw an onrush of state activism that would establish the long-term features of Japan's imperial state. Continental influences undergirded much of daily life now, from rice-growing techniques to the writing system. The native faith, Shintō, competed with the foreign import, Buddhism, for state patronage. Administrative structures had become relatively well ordered, grounded in a combination of domestic and foreign ideas. And the Yamato clan ruled over the archipelago's center as sun-descended kings,[20] assisted by other influential and ambitious families. It seemed time, as one of the edicts suggested, to establish a permanent capital.

CHAPTER 2

Emperors and Aristocrats: Rule by Law and Taste (645–1160)

More than 17,000 people packed the courtyard of Nara's grand new temple, the Tōdaiji, to dedicate a Buddhist statue in the spring of 752. With good reason, for this was no ordinary statue. Rising more than sixty feet from its pedestal, the Daibutsu, or Great Buddha, was made of some three million pounds of metal, contributed by more than 350,000 people, and covered with gold.[1] It sat in a cavernous wooden sanctuary, 150 feet high and 300 feet long, surrounded by a blue-tiled roof, white walls, and lacquered pillars. And it looked out, benignly, on an audience that included the reigning empress Kōken, along with her father, the powerful retired emperor Shōmu, and guests from across the continent.

The celebrants had to wonder what had happened to Japan. A century earlier, the country had not even had a permanent capital. Its rulers had governed from modest halls in hilly Asuka, fifteen miles south of Nara; control of the throne was in dispute. Now, the Tōdaiji ceremony bespoke not just power but splendor and permanence, not just the emergence of Buddhism as an official religion but the emperor's dominance over a large bureaucracy. And the government had located itself in a city of perhaps 100,000 people, modeled after the Chinese capital of Chang'an. The Yamato clan was in total control (at least so it seemed on this dedication day), presiding over a flourishing cultural life and government that would set standards for generations to come.

The change had not, however, come easily. If the early 600s had seen the emergence of the Yamato line under Suiko and Shōtoku Taishi, the mid-600s had produced an explosion of infighting within that line. "Great reforms" notwithstanding, the Soga overthrow precipitated a generation of violence in which one ambitious family then another challenged the throne, and peoples far to the east of Asuka sang plaintively: "Watching the enemy, while going through the woods...we fought, but now we are starving."[2] The culmination of the struggles came in 672, when the king Temmu established himself in power after a brutal civil war and then, with his wife/successor Jitō, launched a series of centralizing reforms that turned the imperial state into something beyond the imaginings even of Suiko and Shōtoku. Driven partly by fear of an invasion from expansive new dynasties in China and Korea and partly by a determination to solidify the control of the ruling line, Temmu and Jitō pushed through programs in the late 600s that made an emperor-centered, Chinese-style administrative structure permanent.

Temmu first strengthened Japan's military forces, creating an army of draftees and placing regional units under the heads of loyal families, whose court ranks were based on how closely they were related to the throne. He also began compiling the Asuka Kiyomihara Code, Japan's first set of joint legal and administrative regulations, confirming kingly prerogatives and bringing greater regularity to government. And he and Jitō went further than their predecessors in asserting his clan's divine origins. Though the records are not entirely clear, Temmu appears to have started the custom of issuing commands under the religious title Manifest Deity, and Jitō, who claimed that Temmu had descended from the sun goddess, is regarded as the first ruler to have used the title today translated as emperor: *tennō*, Heavenly Sovereign.

Accompanying this rise in imperial dominance was a shift in Japan's relations with the continent. In 661, a decade before Temmu's ascendance, a large Japanese fleet had sailed for Korea, intending to support pro-Japanese elements then contending for control of the peninsula. The fleet met with disaster, however, at the hands of a combined Chinese-Korean force off the southwestern Korean coast; as the chronicles described it, "Many of our men were thrown into the water and drowned, and our ships were unable to maneuver. Commander Echi no Takatsu prayed to heaven for victory, gnashed his teeth in anger...and died in battle."[3] That defeat brought overseas military activities to an end—for nearly a millennium. Japan's rulers also halted diplomatic and study missions for several decades, convinced that defense must take precedence over expansion. They still would model their institutions on China and employ Korean immigrants as advisers, craftsmen, and farmers, but they would not spend money on foreign adventures.

The most visible evidence of increasing centralization was the construction of a permanent capital city. Earlier palaces had typically been abandoned when a ruler left the throne. Under Jitō, a site just north of Asuka called Fujiwarakyō was selected by *feng shui* practitioners to become an enduring seat of government in 694. Modeled after Chinese capitals, it was laid out on a grid, with the palace at the north, seven broad streets running north-south, and twelve other avenues running east-west. It had canals, bridges, temples, parks, and markets, and as many as 40,000 residents. When it burned down early in the eighth century, after housing the governments of three successive emperors, however, it was not rebuilt.

In its place, the country established its first permanent capital, Nara, in 710. The site was selected by the reigning empress, Gemmei, in consultation with Fujiwara Fuhito, head of the family that had become the emperors' most influential advisors. Laid out, once again, on a grid with the palace at the north, it covered seventy-two square blocks, stretched eight miles in circumference, and eventually boasted a population of 100,000. Within it were forty Buddhist temples, a 130-foot-wide avenue running south from the palace, markets bustling with glassware, flutes, and foodstuffs from as far away as Chang'an and Persia, and streets filled with visitors from across Asia. Except for the fact that they felt no need to build a city wall, the builders adhered to Chinese styles in everything, from the placement of the palace to the layout of the streets: remarkable evidence of the respect with which Japan's rulers continued to hold the Middle Kingdom. Nara would serve as capital through eight imperial reigns (four female, four male), remaining the seat of government for seventy-five years and producing a plethora of new law codes, religious practices, and cultural styles. It appears to have been during these years that people began referring to their realm as Nihon.

Nara's success sprang in part from a series of remarkable and interesting rulers. The first two, both women, oversaw the beginning of copper mining, the first minting of coins, and the issuance of both the great Yōrō legal code and the *Nihon shoki*. Empress Kōken sat on the throne twice, first when the Great Buddha was dedicated and then during a darker time in the 760s, when the ambitious Buddhist priest Dōkyō won her affections and nearly stole the throne. The most influential Nara emperor was Shōmu, a son-in-law of Fujiwara Fuhito, who took the throne in 724 and dominated official life for more than thirty years, even though he abdicated in 749. Shōmu was an activist administrator who proclaimed the absolute authority of the *tennō*. "It is We who possess the wealth of the land," he proclaimed in 743; "it is We who possess all the power in the land."[4] To make that proclamation reality, he sent military excursions to the north, into the southern Emishi regions, as well as into areas still incompletely controlled in Kyushu. He became the first ruler to wear Chinese-style monarchical robes. And he did more than anyone since Shōtoku to define the relationship between state authority and religion.

Imbued with a fervent faith in both Shintō and Buddhism, Shōmu believed that successful rule depended on the ruler's virtuous behavior, a belief that was reinforced by a series of natural disasters and economic problems in the 730s, including a smallpox epidemic estimated to have taken the lives of up to 70 percent of the population in some regions, including all four of Fuhito's sons.[5] Interpreting those calamities as punishment for his own profligate ways and moved by the example of his pious wife, who was admired for opening medical clinics and caring for the needy, he threw himself into the promotion of Buddhism. He built the Great Buddha, pressuring 2.6 million people (nearly half of Japan's population) to make donations to pay for its erection, and conscripting resentful, sometimes rebellious, peasants to do the construction work. He also sponsored monasteries and nunneries, gave rice fields to favored temples, ordered each province to build a temple, and had block-printed scriptures—one of the world's first examples of printing—distributed and read across the country. Nor did he slight Shintō. He offered prayers to the *kami* (god-spirits) and erected a shrine to the Shintō deity Hachiman outside the Tōdaiji courtyard. After generations of rivalry, Buddhist and Shintō adherents were encouraged to support each other as part of a complementary religious system that would come to be called Ryōbu (two-facet) Shintō.

Nara's most important contribution to Japanese history may have been the completion of a governing structure known as the *ritsuryō* system, or the system of penal and civil codes. The various seventh-century attempts at refining and codifying laws culminated now in an intricate set of regulations that would influence Japanese government for a millennium. The twenty-volume Yōrō codes were drafted in 718, based on a now lost set of laws from 701 called Taihō. Drawn up under Fujiwara Fuhito's supervision and divided into administrative and penal categories, they attempted to apply the Tang governing principles to Japanese institutions, while demonstrating by their very creation that Japan was independent from China.

The codes' central goal was to support a hierarchical, nationwide social and administrative system, with the *tennō* at the top and the government at the center. Power flowed from the emperor, who was served by the Council of State, the Council on Shrine Affairs, and great numbers of central officials who in turn supervised lesser officeholders in sixty-six *kuni* (provinces) and more than 500 districts. Officials were ranked according to their positions. Taxes or tributes were levied according to a complex formula that distributed land units to households on the basis of how many adult men, women, children, and servants lived in them—the assumption being that all land belonged to the emperor, who had the right to distribute it. A regular census would serve as the basis for reallocating land and updating tax registers.

Family lives also were regulated; only men were allowed to file for divorce, but women with children were allowed to remarry after a husband was "detained abroad for five years," or after three years if he ran away.[6] A Ministry of Military Affairs oversaw a national army. Another bureaucracy administered shrines and temples. On the penal side, penalties were harsher for commoners than for officials and priests, with punishments ranging from whipping or beating for lesser offenses to jail, banishment, and death. The Council of State could issue a death sentence, but lower officials could merely have people beaten.

The *ritsuryō* regulations were too complex to be followed fully for very long. Actual landholding patterns differed widely from the codes' detailed allotment system, and reallocations occurred less and less frequently as time passed. Taxes were unevenly assessed, as people cheated or found loopholes. But the codes had a lasting impact. They reinforced the principle of hierarchy, both human and geographical, while instilling respect for the rule of law. And they formed the basic legal framework that was used well into the medieval era. Perhaps most important, they showed that while Chinese approaches to government might be lifted up as the norm, traditional customs and values remained potent. In contrast to China, the *ritsuryō* system provided for no exam system to recruit officials. Nor could Japan's sun-descended emperors lose their right to rule, as they could in China. All women over the age of six received land grants, whereas only married women received land in China. And the establishment of a powerful Council on Shrine Affairs had no Chinese counterpart.

Another contrast between official expressions of how things should be and local reality lay in the lives of commoners. On the one hand, farmers were tied more fully than ever to the emerging state system, as the Nara government built highways to each of the country's major regions to facilitate interchange and control. There were seven such roads, extending as far south as Dazaifu in Kyushu and into the frontiers of the north. These roads made it easier to send troops, to distribute official communications, and to collect taxes, and they made it harder for people in distant regions to ignore the demands of the *ritsuryō* system. On the other hand, the highways gave powerful evidence to those who traveled them that local life was more dynamic and varied than capital stereotypes might have suggested.

In the view of the rich and powerful, peasants were poor and inferior, existing to provide food and taxes, nothing more. Nor was that view entirely wrong, for farmers knew much of hardship. Their taxes largely paid the government's way. They had to provide food and shelter for an average of thirteen people per household. And they, more than others, understood the dual capriciousness of nature and the bureaucracy, vulnerable as they were to illness and even starvation when the weather became bad or tax collectors turned harsh. Tax and land records show that a rising class of moneylenders in the Nara countryside got rich by exploiting poor farmers; they also show an eruption of rural vagrancy, as families fled to unknown regions to avoid debts and taxes. "No fire sends up smoke" at the peasant's hearth, said a poetic provincial official; "a spider spins its web" in the cooking pot, "with not a grain to cook."[7]

Poverty and difficulty, however, did not indicate passivity or inferiority; nor did they tell the entire story. The sources that describe the farmers' plight also show people struggling, resisting, and playing—often quite vigorously. The numerous laws against vagrancy—including a stipulation in the Yōrō code that "when a household absconds, the group shall be responsible for its pursuit"—suggest that farmers did more than complain; many responded to trouble by seeking a fresh start in a new location or by finding ways to avoid taxes. A frustrated eighth-century court official noted: "Cultivators flee to the four corners of the realm, avoid taxes and labor service, and become dependents of princely and ministerial households....Many cultivators in the realm abandon their official place of residence and wander as they please."[8] Others emigrated to the frontier, sometimes in groups of a thousand or more. Then there were those who protested, creating troubles that reached into Nara itself. An edict in 731 complained that rebellious ruffians "numbered thousands and intimidated the superstitious people."[9] And stories of quarrels between commoners and officials were legion; one official named Tatsumaro reportedly killed himself when he could no longer stand the tension involved in balancing the emperor's demands for revenue with the farmers' complaints.[10] Peasants may not have been organized enough to change the system, but neither did they take hardship passively.

Another sign of commoner agency lay in the peasants' responses to popular Buddhism. By the early 700s, crowds in many regions were flocking to sermons by a number of self-appointed priests without ties to established temples. The most prominent of these was Gyōki, the charismatic, unconventional son of a Korean immigrant family who propagated Buddhist doctrines that offered salvation to all. Until his death in 749, at age eighty-one, he attracted huge numbers of followers throughout the Kinai region, reportedly preaching to as many as 10,000 at a time—and healing people, building bridges, and opening new rice lands. The official chronicles said that people "would compete with one another in running to honor him," and that those who "rushed to follow him, yearning to become lay priests, numbered in the thousands."[11] The authorities accused him of raising too much money and spreading confusion, but he was too popular to be stopped, and Shōmu eventually endorsed his emphasis on good works and enlisted his help in gathering support for the Great Buddha.

In addition to providing a permanent capital and a foundation for the *ritsuryō* system, Nara also nourished a golden age in culture, as the emperors threw their resources into creating a city—and a government—as grand as that in China. Architectural marvels in themselves, the city's temples also were rich repositories of art, particularly of Buddhist sculpture. While the Great Buddha was massive, few thought it beautiful. Many of the smaller sculptures, by contrast, combined a naturalism and a grace that later generations would try to emulate. The court also encouraged music, dance, and acrobatics, with a Court Music Bureau promoting the private study of instrumental music and the public performance of *gagaku* ("elegant music"), an enduring classical form that utilized flutes (including the *shakuhachi*), mouth organs, gongs, drums, lutes, and the thirteen-stringed *koto*. Significantly, many of the court's best-loved songs and dances also incorporated popular, even bawdy, materials from the villages.

Even more impressive than the visual and performing arts was poetry. Although the period's earliest writings, the *Kojiki* and *Nihon shoki*, were in prose, the Nara masterpiece was the *Man'yōshū*, a collection of more than 4,500 poems by women and men from all walks of life, compiled in an effort to emulate China's imperial anthologies of poetry. Although most of the poems were in the thirty-one-syllable form called *tanka* (short poem), some were long and discursive. The content was as varied as the writers. Many wrote about life's impermanence, others about Japan's natural beauty. There were paeans to (and by) sovereigns, verses about travel, musings on the death of loved ones, the seasons, and romantic love, as in this *tanka* by the courtier Lady Kasa:

> If love meant death,
> I would have died,
> Then died again,
> Yea, a thousand times and more.[12]

In contrast with the poetry of later eras when formal rules restricted form and content, the *Man'yōshū* verses were as varied as life itself.

*The pagoda at Kiyomizu temple, founded in Kyoto early in the Heian period,
illustrates the multistoried style typical of pagodas at Japan's Buddhist temples.
Constructed to hold sacred scriptures and relics, the pagoda was thought to be
specially charged with spiritual forces.* Photo by Chris McCooey.

Since neither sophisticated administrative codes nor cultural brilliance assured political tranquility, the decades after Shōmu's death again plunged the regime into conflict. In 769, the monk Dōkyō seemed on the verge of becoming *tennō* until leading courtiers banished him to the north. During the 770s, rival lines of the imperial family used murder and intrigue to get their men on the throne, while temples competed for political influence. And warfare reoccurred continuously in northern Honshu, as Yamato forces tried to subdue the Emishi, who by now were mining iron ore and gold and engaging in trade with the continent as well as with Nara. The end of the Emishi wars would not come until the early ninth century, after the loss of thousands of Japanese troops, when victory was claimed by a general with the daunting title "Field Marshal Conqueror of the Barbarians, Provisional Middle General of the Kon'e Guard, Police Commissioner of Mutsu and Dewa, Junior Fourth Rank Upper, Governor of Mutsu, Chinju Shōgun."[13] Even after that, the Emishi would remain quite independent, a continuing challenge to Yamato claims of unity.

By the time the violence waned, Emperor Kammu and another powerful Fujiwara patron, Momokawa, had moved the capital again, to a supposedly temporary palace area jammed with hastily built structures in Heian, twenty miles north of Nara. The temporary proved durable, however, and over the next millennium the city, which eventually was called Kyoto, served as home to seventy-four emperors.

The four centuries we know as the Heian Period, 794–1185, saw a continuation of the emperor-centered, hierarchical *ritsuryō* system. But competing groups found innovative ways to manipulate that system, and practical authority shifted in these years: first from the emperors to their aristocratic advisors, then to a series of retired emperors, with other groups making serious challenges at times. The overall result was four hundred years of relative peace: a time when rivalries were decided by political maneuvering more often than by violence, and when Nara's cultural sprouts matured into a harvest of exceptional music, art, and literature.

One source of Heian's distinctive culture was Japan's increasing separation from the continent. Relations with Korea became strained in the ninth century, as Japanese officials worried that peninsular officials had expansive designs (one midcentury official memo accused the Koreans of "evil intentions" and said that visitors from there "offer no gifts as tribute and spy on state affairs under the guise of commerce").[14] Further west, China's Tang dynasty had by then passed its peak, weakening the Middle Kingdom's allure even as Japan's officials and style-setters grew more self-confident about their own tastes and traditions. The court stopped writing

Chinese-style histories in 887, and in 894, it discontinued its official embassies to China. The government also began trying harder to control private travel to and from the continent, setting up an office at Dazaifu in northern Kyushu to regulate foreign interchange. As a result, most contacts took the form now of priestly pilgrimages and private trade, which developed fairly extensively after the tenth century—or of Korean and Chinese pirates plundering Japanese silk and other luxury items. Migration from Asia slowed to a trickle. Perhaps most significant of all, the Japanese developed their own phonetic writing symbols, called *kana*, creating a complex system that blended Chinese characters with *kana* and, in the process, fueled an explosion of writing. While the Japanese never cut themselves off wholly from Asia, the tendency toward independence was undeniable.

The most dramatic political changes resulted from the emperors' gradual loss of influence, even though they remained on the throne. The Yamato *tennō* still controlled the system in the early 800s, but by midcentury their Fujiwara advisers had maneuvered themselves into power, dispensing patronage and manipulating the *ritsuryō* system in a way that left the sovereigns with prestige but limited clout. Indeed, by the middle of the tenth century, the northern or Hokke branch of the Fujiwara had become absolutely dominant in the capital. All the while, officials and commoners in the countryside grew less dependent on the center, generally paying their taxes and providing corvee labor but taking charge of local affairs: punishing miscreants in their own ways, and dealing as they could with the three-year famine/epidemic cycles that kept the population static across these centuries at about six million.

The Fujiwara family members' culture and extravagance—their luxurious residences, patronage of the arts, elegant lovemaking—did more than anything else to set them apart from the other power-holders of Japanese history, but the key to their ascendance lay in their ability to play a hard political game. Late in the ninth and early in the tenth centuries, for example, when two emperors attempted to counter the Fujiwara's hold on power by giving high office to Michizane, of the rival Sugawara family, the Fujiwara responded brutally, questioning his loyalty to the throne and having him banished to northern Kyushu, where he lived under house arrest and complained, in verse:

> Farm children brought me vegetables,
> And my kitchen helper made me a thin gruel.
> I wasted away like a lonely crane bereft of its mate.[15]

He was dead within two years, possibly of malnutrition, and people in Heian began blaming each new fire or windstorm on his angry ghost. But his experience made them think thrice before challenging the Fujiwara.

One source of the family's control was their skill in nurturing powerful allies and placing their own people in key offices. They drew support from several of the country's most powerful temples, including the Kōfukuji in Nara. The family also managed, from the mid-800s onward, to have its men named regents to most rulers, first to minors sitting on the throne and then, after the 880s, to adult emperors. And they took charge of the Heian's Office of Police. By the tenth century, they controlled the city's security forces, its board of appointments, and most of its key administrative posts, as well as the emperor's calendar and decision-making process.

Equally important, the Fujiwara married their daughters off carefully. Following earlier traditions, they made every effort to place Fujiwara offspring in the palace as wives of promising princes. Women no longer ascended the throne in this era, and gender roles became more sharply delineated; women were now denied the right to hold most offices or participate in government ceremonies. Exclusion from the public arena did not render women powerless, however; it simply meant that they had to shape affairs less formally, as mothers and spouses of influential men—who typically moved into the wife's family residence on marriage. Fujiwara Onshi, the *kokumo* (mother of the nation, or queen mother), for instance, forced her way into her emperor-son's bedroom to demand that he support her brother Michinaga as regent. "The imperial mother," said a tenth-century official, "makes affairs of the court solely her own."[16] The best known imperial mother was Fujiwara Shōshi, who influenced five emperors—two sons, two grandsons, and a great-grandson—in the eleventh century and included among her ladies-in-waiting Murasaki Shikibu, the author of the *Tale of Genji*, which is considered the world's first novel.

The Fujiwara also used the Heian era's emerging landholding system to strengthen their hold on power. The Nara principle that all land belonged to the emperor required regular censuses and land reassignments so that taxes could be assessed. By the early 800s, that process had become too cumbersome for effective enforcement. Censuses were discontinued, reallocations declined, and local control of land expanded. Concomitantly, a practice that had begun in the Nara years—the accumulation of "private" estates, called *shōen,* by temples and aristocratic families—gathered force. Under the early *ritsuryō* system, the idea of permanent ownership was given a foothold when religious institutions and landholding families were promised enduring title to land they reclaimed from forests, as long as they paid taxes. Now, in Heian, these groups competed energetically in finding new ways to secure permanent lands: as gifts for services rendered to the emperor, as rewards for holding certain offices, or by taking over the lands of poor farmers, often

Murasaki Shikibu's Tale of Genji, *written about 1000 CE, describes the brilliant court life of the Heian years. This painting, taken from a thirteenth-century edition of Murasaki's other important literary contribution, her diary, depicts elaborately attired court ladies with long hair, painted eyebrows, and rosebud-red lips. They care for children and wait on men, who typically wore hats, from within a curtained enclosure.* TNM Image Archives.

in exchange for a promise that the peasant's rents would be lower than taxes had been. By the middle of the Heian period, most of these estates had become tax free, often even free from entry by government inspectors or other officials. Needless to say, the vast expansion of this system strained government income. But it gave the Fujiwara, who owned thousands of *shōen*, the financial base to dominate politics.

The *shōen* system also engendered growing independence and diversity in the provinces. Since estate managers answered to Heian-based families or temples rather than to the central government, they were able to act with increasing autonomy in their many duties: directing the estate's annual planting and harvesting, purchasing and selling its products, securing housing for cultivators and workers, and communicating with estate owners in the capital. Temples and shrines also became heavily involved in local commercial affairs under the *shōen* system, sending out agents to market expensive goods and loaning money at high interest rates to poor and rich patrons alike. A class of rich farmers emerged outside the *shōen* too, as collaborators with local authorities in loaning money or assuring that their neighbors' taxes were paid. The result of all this activity was the growth of stronger, more assertive provincial regions and a remarkable spread of commerce, travel, and money-lending.

Evidence of local vibrancy shows up in a variety of mid-Heian records. The archives of Kōzanji temple outside Kyoto, for example, have turned up letters of travelers that describe monks doubling as commercial agents, buying and selling horses for local hunters; landholders competing with each other to secure loans for the spring planting; local patrons "arriving early to get good seats near the stage" at temple dances and promising "to offer congratulatory gifts to the performers"; and low-ranking noble families moving into the provinces and "seizing cultivators' fields to add to their own holdings."[17] Similarly, a late tenth-century complaint by local officials in Owari, some eighty miles northeast of Heian, describes not only a complex highway system that a governor was failing to maintain but an impressive array of local products that he was requisitioning as taxes. He is "cheating us," the document read, "by taking silk taffeta, handwoven hemp cloth...oil, China grass (*karamushi*) cloth, Indian madder, and silk floss." To meet his demands, the petition said, "we have to sell the property of our ancestors and to endanger the survival of our children and grandchildren."[18] The growing provincial potency was demonstrated by the governor's removal from office the year after the complaint was lodged.

In the capital itself, the Fujiwara influence peaked in the early eleventh century. Although these decades saw more than their share of provincial unrest and an unusual number of palace fires—some accidental, some set by thieves—they are regarded as the glory time of the regent Michinaga, a man known for his erudition, poor health, and love affairs, along with his determined manipulation of the levers of power. He ran society not by bold policies or efficient government but by controlling the web of networks around the throne. He was father-in-law to three emperors and grandfather to two. He was related by blood to most of the decision-makers. He used his ties to direct the interminable backroom discussions that characterized decision-making. "This world, I think, is indeed my world," he wrote in a 1018 poem. "Like the full moon I shine, uncovered by any cloud."[19] Emperors conducted ceremonies and centered things; officials discussed and consulted; Michinaga dominated.

It should not surprise us that Michinaga expressed his self-satisfaction in verse, because art and culture experienced a heyday during his years. The aristocrats made up less than half a percent of the populace, but they were highly literate, educated in Chinese literature and thought as well as in the growing body of Japanese writings. They had sufficient income from the *shōen* to construct fine residences and spend time in the arts. And they knew that literary and artistic skill would gain them as much respect and influence as political acumen would. The result was the emergence of a sophisticated urban populace who produced one of history's richest feasts of dance, architecture, painting, music, and literature, all governed by refined aesthetic standards. For a society so recently illiterate—indeed for any society—the output was stunning.

One characteristic of Heian culture was the artists' emancipation from Chinese models. People continued to admire China, and men did most of their public writing in Chinese. Official documents, too, were composed in Chinese. By the tenth century, however, most things cultural had taken on a more Japanese hue. In architecture, for example, Michinaga's son Yorimichi defied formalistic Chinese styles in the 1050s when he constructed the era's representative building, the Phoenix Hall at the Byōdōin temple southeast of Kyoto, surrounding the building with water and flanking the central hall with long, delicate, airy wings. Native tastes were also exemplified in the new Japanese-style paintings called *yamato-e* (Yamato pictures), which typically were done on the sliding walls and folding screens of aristocrats' homes and graced by poems written in flowing calligraphy.

Even more original—and Japanese—were the late Heian *emakimono*, or picture scrolls. Typically thirty or forty feet long, they narrated stories with pictures and (sometimes) writing when unrolled from right to left. Some of them were religious; the most remarkable were secular, sometimes jocular. The ethereal Genji Scroll, illustrating the elaborately dressed figures of Murasaki's *Tale of Genji*, is generally regarded as the best. More fun is the cartoon-like animal scroll, credited to a priest named Toba, that portrays squirrels, rabbits, frogs, and monkeys acting as priests, officials, and even Buddha himself. Chinese visitors disdained this sort of work and continued to refer to the Japanese as provincial barbarians, but the paintings revealed a growing self-confidence and a level of artistry that would be much admired by later generations.

Heian cultural life was also marked by an overweening religiosity. The court sponsored two sects, Tendai and Shingon, both of which spread their esoteric teachings from mountaintop centers. But while aristocrats generally followed one or both of these, they rarely stopped there. Like the commoners, most also took up a personalized mixture of practices related to the Shintō worship of *kami*, the aestheticism of a new mountain religious order called Shugendō, and the magic of folk

One of the late Heian period's most enduring works, this animal scroll, attributed to the priest Toba, playfully used frogs, rabbits, and other animals to poke fun at the pretensions of priests and officials. TNM Image Archives.

religion. They were also influenced by the rise of Amida Buddhism, a doctrine that promised entry into the Pure Land of the Western Paradise to anyone who had faith in the compassionate Buddha Amida. Monks from the Tendai center at Mount Hiei, just north of Kyoto, became advocates of this people-oriented faith, too, as did Kūya, a charismatic priest in the tradition of Gyōki, who traversed the country helping the poor and preaching salvation. All of these religions had two things in common: they were pervasive, and they were eclectic. Although officials liked to organize religion into distinct doctrines and sects, the Heian citizenry—aristocrats and commoners, priests and laity—engaged in a mix of practices that ignored categories.

These religions played a key role in energizing the Heian arts. Temples provided a site for many of the era's finest buildings and pagodas, including the Phoenix Hall. Priests turned out paintings on religious themes—Amida descending to earth on a host of clouds, bodhisattvas spreading enlightenment, the abstract geometric forms called mandalas, which represented all of the elements of the cosmos—as a means of explaining doctrine to the uninitiated. Monks such as Kūkai, the founder of Shingon Buddhism, made calligraphy into a significant art form. Sculptors turned out a range of Buddhist figures, from fierce guardian deities to gentle representations of a tranquil, seated Amida. The greatest innovation in Heian sculpture was the use of wood: small images made of a single piece in the early years, large and lifelike images in the later Heian years, crafted by joining several pieces of wood together.

A rising emphasis on the subdued and the simple as the essence of beauty may have been the most distinctly Japanese feature of Heian aristocratic culture. Certainly the era's aesthetic sensitivities encompassed colorful and lively things. Court ceremonies included grand promenades. Palace women wore multilayered court robes, reddened their lips, blackened their teeth, and whitened their faces, and men dressed extravagantly. Moreover, several literary masterpieces exuded earthy wit, some of it sexual. The *Pillow Book* of Lady Sei Shōnagon, for example, includes a lover who "starts snoring" in its list of "hateful things," and adds: "fleas, too, are very hateful."[20] But it was the appreciation of gentle emotions and quiet elegance that dominated Heian literature and art. To be respected, one had to demonstrate good taste, write poetry in a polished hand, and understate things. A key concept in the Heian cultural vocabulary was *miyabi*, or courtly refinement. Another was *mono no aware*, or sensitivity to the pathos of things, to life's fragility and thus its beauty. The writer Ki Tsurayuki caught the essence of Heian aesthetic tastes in his famous description of poetry. "Japanese poetry," he wrote, "has for its seed the human heart.... Who among men does not compose poetry on hearing the song of the nightingale among the flowers, or the cries of the frog who lives in the water?"[21]

These standards were set by women as much as by men; for Heian cultural life was driven by both genders, and its literary scene was dominated by women. The era's written output was voluminous, including collections of tales, travel narratives, gossipy histories, autobiographies, and court diaries, with women producing the best known works. The *Pillow Book*, which introduced the miscellany genre, is an example. It gives us nearly 200 of Lady Sei's witty essays on everything from snow-covered peasant huts to priests' attire, from "things that fall from the sky" (hail and snow) to "things that should be short" ("the speech of a young girl") and things that are "squalid" ("the inside of a cat's ear").[22] It also provides sharp insight into daily life at the court. While men were more prominent in poetry, even there, one of the most popular writers was the shadowy Ono Komachi, who became legendary for her poems and her beauty. A major contributor to the era's first major anthology, the *Kokinshū*, she describes a range of powerful human experiences, including the nights when "my breast throbs / my heart is ravaged by flame" because a lover has failed to show up.[23]

The pride of Heian literature was fiction, especially the masterpiece that defined the era, the eleventh-century *Tale of Genji*, which runs to more than a thousand pages. Most of the story describes the life and dalliances of the "shining Genji," a courtier known for his great learning, his elegant attire, his skill in the arts, and his love affairs. The novel's power lay partly in its exquisite illustrations of *miyabi*: delicate courtesans making snowballs on a winter evening, flowers climbing the walls of a poor woman's home, Genji writing love notes on a tree leaf. It also illustrated the complex power relationships between men and women. And it showcased the era's love of poetry; it contains 795 poems. Moralists sometimes have derided Genji and his etiquette-obsessed court as lecherous and avaricious. More typical are those who see him as the epitome of a world that not only preserved a broad peace for centuries but produced an exquisite, creative array of arts and literature.

During the late eleventh century, the imperial family took back political power—not through its reigning emperors, but through family members who would ascend the throne, then abdicate a few years later and retire to a monastery, where they could operate from behind the scenes in a system known as *insei* (literally, "cloistered government"). When Gosanjō became emperor in 1068 as the first sovereign born to a non-Fujiwara mother in nine generations, he instituted an aggressive program to get control of the private-estate system back into the emperor's hands. Though he died only five years later, before he could accomplish all he desired, his policies were replicated and extended by three successors, all of whom dominated government from retirement. For the next seventy-five years, the *insei* accumulated many private estates for the imperial family and then used the revenues from those estates to cement alliances with the newly important Taira and Minamoto military families, and restore the imperial line to dominance.

One thing that kept the *insei* from gaining even fuller control was the tumultuous nature of public life after the mid–eleventh century, which spurred a sharp decline in the *ristusyō* structures. The Fujiwara did not give up easily, though many of their fights were among themselves now, with a rival clan branch that had roots in the Emishi dominating a rich and sophisticated center at Hiraizumi, hundreds of miles north of Heian, for a century after the 1080s. The retired emperors also were threatened by the Buddhist establishment, which was concentrated in the many Tendai temples that had been built on the slopes of Mount Hiei. Buddhist temples had always fought with each other over issues like land control and the right to ordain priests. Beginning in the late eleventh century, however, the fights between Hiei temples grew bitterly violent, leading to repeated attacks by the temples' armed units, with widespread burning of buildings and significant loss of lives. The temples also sent increasing numbers of armed monks into the Heian streets to demand privileges from the government. While the conflicts did not threaten the existence of the *insei*, they made it increasingly difficult for it to exercise control.

The later Heian years also faced the government with spreading violence in the provinces: for example, an effort in the 1030s by the warrior Taira Tadatsune to wrest control of a large region north and east of present-day Tokyo, two far northern struggles against the Emishi in the last half of the century over land and control issues, and constant problems with Inland Sea piracy early in the 1100s. Heian Japan had, until now, been a land of relative peace, a place where culture and refinement trumped martial skills, a country whose political struggles were carried out by intermarrying and maneuvering, not by fighting. It is not surprising, then, that these disturbances precipitated predictions of doom. Nor is it surprising that the retired emperors found it necessary, more and more, to seek assistance from networks of military families that had begun developing in provincial Japan. Lacking an army themselves, worried about the Fujiwara, and threatened by religious and provincial violence, they saw little option by the early twelfth century but to begin turning to the Taira and Minamoto warriors for help. It was an understandable move. Midcentury developments, however, would prove it a dangerous one.

Warriors:
The Long Rise (1160–1550)

A n old Japanese tale depicts the warrior Kumagai Naozane fighting a solitary horseman on an Inland Sea beach in 1184. Ripping off the horseman's helmet, he discovered a teenager "so handsome that he could find no place to strike" and had nearly decided to spare him when he saw fifty of his own fellows approaching. Certain that they would be merciless, he decided he had no choice. "In tears, he took the head," the story tells us, only to discover that the lad, named Atsumori, was carrying the flute whose melodies had wafted out from the enemy camp that morning. "After that, Naozane thought increasingly of becoming a monk."[1]

This tale, one of scores in the *Tales of Heike* that blind, wandering minstrels recited during Japan's medieval centuries, has long been a children's favorite. The episode's primary import at the time, however, lay in its evidence that new historical currents were flowing. In Atsumori's death we see unbridled warfare, of a sort unimaginable a century earlier; we see warriors obsessed with beauty (not only was he handsome; he wore makeup); and we see soldiers seeking solace in religion. We also see intimations of an era when the center of national activity would change, when the emperors' and officials' power would be usurped by those in the hinterlands—where rivals sought influence through swords, farmers congregated in villages and produced new crops, merchants and traders spurred a remarkable commercial revolution, and Zen priests introduced wholly new artistic forms. These medieval years would also see renewed engagement with the continent.

Notions that change was afoot were encouraged by an upsurge of violence late in the 1150s, giving Heian (now called Kyoto or "capital city") its first experience with full-fledged military clashes between pretenders for power. The warrior clans that had begun asserting themselves in the late Heian years moved onto center stage now, with the Taira and Minamoto families vying for control. After two crucial battles, the Taira became ascendant in Kyoto in 1160, adopting the ruling techniques that had proved effective for the Fujiwara and the *insei*. The family head, Kiyomori, commandeered key offices, secured high court ranks, married his daughters into the aristocratic lines, and amassed wealth through trade and land acquisition. Although he never achieved the strength of earlier power-holders, he dominated capital life for two decades. He also alienated people with an abrasive approach that included the arrest of the retired emperor Goshirakawa in 1179 for an anti-Taira conspiracy, and the temporary shifting of the capital to Fukuhara on the Inland Sea, where "the roar of the waves made a constant din, and the salt winds were of a terrible severity."[2]

Kiyomori's harsh measures created enemies, and by 1180 a nation-wide conflagration known as the Genpei War was under way, led by the thirty-three-year-old Minamoto Yoritomo, whom Kiyomori had exiled as a child to Kamakura, some 300 miles to the east. Fighting was brutal but sporadic at first, with few clearcut victories, as rival Minamoto chiefs struggled against each other as much as against the Taira. Gradually, however, the Minamoto became more unified, and in 1185 they triumphed in a climactic sea battle at Dannoura off Honshu island's western tip. According to the *Tales of the Heike*, the battle ended when Lady Nii picked up Kiyomori's grandson, the eight-year-old emperor

A scroll painting depicts the pivotal 1160 Heiji battle in which Minamoto family horsemen set fire to the palace and kidnapped former emperor Goshirakawa. Soon thereafter, the Taira family recaptured Goshirakawa, defeated the Minamoto, and took control of Heian, thus bringing an end to Fujiwara family power. Photograph © 2010, Museum of Fine Arts, Boston (*Night Attack on the Sanjō Palace, from the Illustrated Scrolls of the Events of the Heiji Era*, Fenollosa-Weld Collection, 11.4000).

Antoku, and jumped into the sea with the declaration: "In the depths of the Ocean we have a Capital!"[3]

For the next 150 years, the government had two centers, with the imperial clan dominating civil affairs in Kyoto while the warrior families in Kamakura—first the Minamoto and then their in-laws, the Hōjō—commanded the newly empowered warrior networks. Although the military alliances provided a stiff new challenge, official life in Kyoto remained much as it had been for centuries: officials there collected the taxes; the court appointed officials and adjudicated civilian disputes; the emperors dispensed ranks. And courtiers patronized the arts, though in reduced circumstances. A century after the Genpei War, Kyoto's prominent Lady Nijō described the court ceremonies that marked a shogun's visit; they included streets lined with observers, officials in green and white robes, block on block of "smartly dressed" military lords, and "a splendid ceremonial viewing of horses." She was impressed by the splendor yet said "these events saddened me with memories of distant days at court."[4]

The reason for the faded glory lay, of course, in Kamakura. While Yoritomo's initial goal had been limited to assuring himself control of the warriors in his own region, the Genpei War turned him into a national peacekeeper. By the 1200s, his administrative offices were assigning lands, providing security, and adjudicating disputes among warrior families throughout Japan. They also had devised mechanisms to ensure Kyoto's cooperation, much as the Fujiwara aristocrats had done in earlier centuries. The difference now was that the emperors had to work not with Kyoto noblemen but with eastern warriors, a rising class called samurai or *bushi*.

This new arrangement had a number of practical consequences. First, after half a millennium of Kinai dominance, Japan had a rival power center in the east, a city hewed from the coastal mountainsides at great cost to the forested environment. Second, power struggles were frequently handled by violence. Yoritomo wiped out rivals within his own family—including his younger half-brother, the legendary hero Yoshitsune—with a brutality that brooked no sentiment. In 1189, he eradicated the northern Fujiwara branch at Hiraizumi. And when the retired emperor Gotoba challenged the Kamakura government in 1221, Yoritomo's widow, Hōjō Masako, quashed his rebellion violently and confiscated the lands of his Kyoto supporters. The ostensible goal of the Kamakura administration was to prevent warfare; the reality was that challenges were often settled on the battlefield.

A third result of dual rule was the continued evolution—or devolution—of the *ritsuryō* system. While the basic concept of rule by court-oriented law continued, the new military rulers initiated processes that would, in time, destroy traditional governance. One sign of change was the name Yoritomo gave to his Kamakura headquarters: *bakufu* (tent government), a term that traditionally had denoted the offices of a general sent to fight the Emishi or other "barbarian" groups. Neither that name nor the title *shogun* (generalissimo), which Yoritomo took in 1192, held much prestige at the time; indeed, Yoritomo was more interested in securing court ranks than in being called shogun. But the application of military terms to important administrative offices suggested the fundamental changes under way. Even more significant was the emergence of new military offices. Kamakura began appointing a *shugo* (constable) over each province to punish criminals and certify families as Minamoto vassals. Even more important, it started naming men and women across Japan to the crucial post of *jitō* (estate steward), making them responsible for administering land, collecting taxes, and enforcing laws at the estate level—and thereby challenging the Kyoto aristocrats' hold on the private estate system.

These new arrangements gave rise, in their turn, to an increasingly diverse population in the countryside. The existence of rival power centers in Kamakura and Kyoto encouraged an expansion of roads and sea routes, which attracted a great traveling population: storytellers, horse dealers, peddlers, and magicians, along with thieves and prostitutes. It was not unusual now to see a blind, itinerant priest standing under an umbrella at a crossroads, reciting popular stories from the *Tales of the Heike* to a provincial crowd. Nor could one miss the constant movements of hunters, craftsmen, and traders who sold their meat and wares to the great temples and the aristocratic city families. The roadsides also provided space for some of Japan's earliest markets and for its first inns with public baths. And they eased travel to and from the coastal villages, where the men made salt and went fishing, while the women prepared the fish, which they then took to the cities for sale. Although officials tended to think of Japan simplistically—as divided between the agricultural and governmental spheres—life along the roads made it clear that things were more complex. The wanderers, the peddlers, the women fishmongers, and the hunters who traveled the country's roads made up a crucial part of thirteenth-century society, spreading fashions and culture even as they provided the goods that made life possible.

One practical feature of the old system that did not change was the deep influence of regents, or people whose titles hid their actual roles. The prime example was Masako, Yoritomo's widow, who exercised real power after he died in 1199, allegedly by falling from a horse. Two sons succeeded him as shogun, but she was in charge. She dominated Kamakura offices, issued instructions to troops, and confirmed landholdings, resorting when necessary to secret plots against the lives of her own children. After her death in 1225, her father's family, the Hōjō, dominated Kamakura for generations, with actual power residing not in the reigning emperor or in the shogun, but in the shogunal regent.

Masako was not the only influential woman of her period. When the thirteenth-century priest-historian Jien described Japan as "a state where 'women are the finishing touches,'"[5] he had in mind both Masako and her Kyoto rival, Fujiwara Kaneko, who shaped many of the court's most important appointments and policies. Another Kyoto woman, Emperor Goshirakawa's concubine Tango Tsubone, was known in the late 1100s for her consummate skill in countering many of Yoritomo's and Masako's schemes. Women were important on the battlefield too; whereas the feats of the legendary woman warrior Tomoe may have been mythical, those of many other female horsemen were solidly historical, even if less dramatic. And under the Kamakura period's major legal codes, the Formulary of Adjudications, women continued to own estates and head families. The era produced fewer prominent female writers, but as in Heian, women colluded with men at the heart of power.

If the sword brought influence to the Minamoto and Hōjō families, it also hastened their demise. By the second half of the 1200s, the Kamakura *bakufu* was in trouble, weakened by factional infighting and the increasing independence of many *jitō*, as well as by many officials' luxurious lifestyles. The difficulties were heightened by Japan's first direct foreign threat in 500 years, when an envoy from the Mongol regime that had overrun Korea and China appeared in Kamakura in 1268 with a message from Kublai Khan purporting to desire "friendly relations" yet warning ominously: "Nobody would wish to resort to arms."[6] When Kamakura ignored several similar requests over the next few years, the Mongols made good on the threat and dispatched several thousand soldiers to Japan in November 1274. The Japanese fought valiantly and then were assisted by a serious storm—what a courtier referred to as "a reverse (easterly) wind" that "must have arisen [as a result of] the protection of the gods"[7]—that sent the Mongols fleeing, minus a third of their men. Over next years, the Hōjō prepared for another invasion by raising new forces and building a twelve-mile-long defensive wall along the northern Kyushu invasion site. When the Mongols returned with even more troops early in the summer of 1281, the Japanese fought the invaders to a draw before nature assisted again, with a typhoon that settled the Mongols' fate.

The Hōjō regime benefited from these victories in the short run. The wartime mobilization broadened its power base and many saw the *kamikaze* (divine winds) as evidence of the gods' protection of Japan and its rulers. In the longer run, however, the invasions undermined the regime. The defense effort drained government coffers, even as it disrupted agricultural production. The demands of *bakufu* allies for compensation after the Mongol battles ended multiplied the economic difficulties. Traditionally, troops had been rewarded with spoils taken from the vanquished, but these invaders left no spoils. So Kamakura was forced to pay its supporters, including the priests who prayed for divine intervention, from its own treasury. When the hard-pressed government finally stopped such payments, disaffection mushroomed. One fighter whose valor had been "proved to the authorities" complained: "I have been left out of the general recognition of merit, and my grief is extreme."[8]

Particularly ominous was a rise in lawlessness in the post-invasion years, typified by the appearance of great numbers of *akutō* or "evil bands" of disaffected people who resorted to military-style violence throughout the countryside, destroying fields, burning houses, and demanding land rights or lower taxes. Coming from both the dispossessed lower classes and the samurai ranks, these bands employed a wide range of weapons—from slingshots and logs to swords and catapults—in an effort to gain redress from money-grubbing temples, government tax collectors, and a host of other offenders. Some of them wore unusual clothing, including the sleeveless kimonos of women and the yellow scarves of the lowest classes. All of them evoked wide fear that the country was approaching a cataclysm.

The Hōjō government struggled on until the 1330s, when another civil war, the Kemmu Restoration, brought it to an end and restored administrative functions to Kyoto. The trigger for the Restoration was the culmination of a long-running succession dispute between rival claimants to the throne. Convinced that one of the imperial rivals, Godaigo, wanted not just the emperor's chair but Kamakura's power, the Hōjō exiled him in 1331 to Oki island off western Honshu. That did not end matters. He escaped the next year and quickly won the support of several warrior families, including the Ashikaga. His new allies first combined to drive the Hōjō from power, and then the Ashikaga turned on the emperor himself, triggering several years of chaotic violence. By 1338, Godaigo again had been vanquished, and Ashikaga Takauji had become shogun. An anonymous observer posted a sign in Kyoto commenting that the day's fads included "assaults in the night, armed robberies, falsified documents, easy women...chopped-off heads, monks who defrock themselves and laymen who shave their heads."[9]

The Kemmu Restoration initiated another shift in Japan's governing structure. Dual government largely vanished now, as the military administration was moved back to Kyoto, to a section of the city called Muromachi. Warfare flourished, and the provinces asserted increasing independence. After midcentury, the Ashikaga family won a wide enough network of military and religious supporters to establish themselves in solid control of the central region, where they created an array of new income-producing schemes and a relatively effective bureaucracy. In 1392, they ended the imperial succession dispute, first brokering a compromise between the rival lines, then reneging and rejecting the Godaigo line's claims. But they were never able to secure a firm grasp in the provinces.

One key to the Muromachi years lay in the Ashikaga's heavy focus on Kyoto, on working with the old civilian rulers and emulating their ways. Mirroring the Fujiwara, the family played marriage politics vigorously. At the same time, they developed an administrative structure in which the Ashikaga family head typically served as shogun, while a *kanrei,* or deputy shogun, from one of three powerful allied families exercised day-to-day power. Since their army was relatively small, they signed agreements with local power holders, some of whom were called *daimyō* (great names), that secured these local lords' allegiance by granting them relative autonomy and the right to retain half of the estate fees they collected. One effect of these policies was that regional military alliances multiplied in the late 1300s; another was that the *jitō* saw their authority decline, as local estate managers felt less compelled to heed Kyoto's demands; yet another was the continuing slippage of Kyoto's influence outside the capital region.

The resultant drop in revenues from private estates caused many difficulties for the *bakufu,* but, ironically, the Kyoto power-holders' search for alternative revenue sources had a salutary economic impact on the country as a whole, spreading the wealth in new ways and encouraging the rise of small-scale capitalism. The old noble families struggled to maintain their revenue flow by turning themselves into financial organizations, loaning out money at high interest rates and charging fees in return for giving protection to emerging merchant groups. The great temples created a variety of schemes to increase income: serving as tax collectors, lending out money at usurious rates, controlling shipping on Lake Biwa to Kyoto's north. The authorities supplemented declining land tax revenues with roadway tolls, fees on temples for the right to ordain priests, and perhaps most important, heavy surcharges on moneylenders. Private families without formal ties to any of the old ruling groups devised money-making schemes of their own. Banking, for example, got its start in this period, and sake brewers flourished. By the 1400s, the Kyoto-Nara region boasted a thousand money-lending firms and breweries. The period even spawned a new word for private businessmen: *utokunin*, which contained the double meaning "virtuous person" and "profit maker."

The most controversial income-producing scheme was enacted by Ashikaga Yoshimitsu, who served as shogun from 1369 until 1395 and then dominated affairs from retirement until his death in 1408. An active administrator, an intimate of emperors, and a lavish spender on buildings such as the gold-covered Kinkakuji villa, he agreed in 1402 that the *bakufu* would dispatch tribute missions to China in exchange for the Ming Dynasty's recognition of Ashikaga supremacy in Japan. Along with a huge shipment of gifts, he sent a statement attributing to Emperor Yongle "the brightness...of the radiant sun"; the Chinese ruler in return called him the "King of Japan." The relationship yielded a significant increase in trade—enough to keep the tribute relationship going for 150 years, even though many Japanese denounced Yoshimitsu for accepting "vassal" status.[10]

Yoshimitsu was probably the strongest of the Ashikaga rulers, and while some of his successors worked assiduously at strengthening the central institutions, the general trend was toward decentralization. Vassal families fought with each other, local rebellions against debt collections and unfair levies spilled into Kyoto, and the most effective of Yoshimitsu's successors was murdered at a banquet in 1441. Affairs reached a crisis during the 1460s under the shogun Yoshimasa, whose love of the arts overshadowed his interest in governing. A Zen priest captured the decade's tone in a diary entry during the spring of 1460. He had seen an old woman carrying a dead child and wailing about greedy officials who would not help her: "While I was still humbly mulling over her sad story, I encountered a group of noblemen out to admire the blossoms. Some sneered at the people in the streets; others swore at the menials in the path of their horses; others laughingly stole blossoms; others, drunkenly singing, drew their swords."[11]

When a dispute over who would be the next shogun arose in the mid-1460s, the regime had few resources to deal with it, and the result was a disastrous war named for the era in which it began: the Ōnin Upheaval. Most of the leading samurai families took part in what can only be called an orgy of violence, burning temples, ransacking shops, massacring hostages, and defiling the dead. By the war's end in 1477, the fighting had moved to the countryside because all vestiges of central control had been destroyed and Kyoto had been wiped out. "For blocks on end," said the conflict's leading chronicler, "birds are the sole sign of life."[12] Ironically, the Upheaval did not even produce a victor. The warring families simply lost their sources of income and influence, while Shogun Yoshimasa retreated to a life of the arts, and his successors followed each other in relatively meaningless fashion. The imperial family descended into poverty.

One figure who benefited from the disaster was the *daimyō* in the countryside. Having replaced the *jitō*, the *shugo*, and the *bakufu* as local power brokers, these lords would take advantage of the empty center to hew out a new age, a *sengoku* (warring states) period in which provincial power was exercised by military chieftains and fighting was almost continuous. The heroic, violent actions of the period's leaders fired the popular imagination for centuries, giving rise to the samurai genre of fiction, film, and *anime*. And the decentralized, warrior-based nature of power later invoked comparisons to European feudalism. In reality, the time had a brutal yet dynamic quality that was unique to itself, an energy that produced new institutions even as it demolished old ones.

For generations, students of this era focused on things that declined: imperial authority, *bakufu* power, the national military clans. Even as those institutions experienced troubles, however, vibrant local forces were producing fresh styles of national life pervasive enough to make the period seminal in Japanese development. Villages became more organized in these years; agriculture and commerce flourished in vibrant and unexpected ways; religion and art took on different forms; living standards rose throughout the countryside. And the source of much of this change was the *daimyō*, who ruled by dominating the lands immediately surrounding him. It was this figure, the local military lord who— along with his allies (or, just as often, his rivals) in farming, religion, and commerce—made the *sengoku* years such an innovative period. He was the one too who gave the era its mystique as a time of insubordination (*gekokujō*), when power sprang from ability rather than pedigree.

Most *sengoku daimyō* lived initially in fortified residences on the plains, but as the era progressed, many built larger, permanent castles on mountain ridges and peaks. Surrounded by trenches and defense towers, these structures foreshadowed the multistoried castles that the great domains used for defense and administration in a more settled time after the early 1600s. Revenues came from trade, commerce, and taxes on farmers in the domain. And security came from the sword, as *sengoku daimyō* marshalled ever-larger armies to defend and expand territory. In time, they began requiring their vassals to move off their own farms and villages and into the domain headquarters, where loyalty could more easily be assured. These rulers also drafted detailed legal codes for their vassals, demonstrating that they believed in rule by law.

Warfare was a constant in these years, but fighting styles changed. After the Ōnin conflict, where most combat had been hand to hand, a typical fief's forces numbered a few hundred; by the mid-1500s, many domains had tens of thousands of fighters. Armies became complex; masses of lightly dressed foot soldiers, called *ashigaru*, were led by elite units of armed horsemen and followed by workers who provided food and supplies. Lighter weapons were developed to facilitate mobility: halberds, pikes, and eventually matchlock guns. A rising mystique of loyalty and discipline laid the foundation for the *bushidō* myth of later centuries. At the same time, the era saw more than its share of

The armor of a typical daimyō *in the warring states period of the late 1400s and early 1500s, with iron bars wrapped in colorful cords, beneath a helmet of lacquer and metal. Though highly effective for defense, the weight of the armor made it impossible for a* daimyō *to participate actively in battle; his role was to sit or stand in a protected place and give directions. TNM Image Archives.*

treachery, as each *daimyō* sought every means to gain an advantage. In an often-repeated story, the warrior Hōjō Sōun of Izu announced that blind people in his region would be killed, as a cover for sending them into neighboring areas as spies.

Many of the medieval era's most significant changes, especially after the 1300s, came in the agricultural sector. Production already had increased in the Kamakura period, thanks to better fertilizers, sharper tilling instruments, and the introduction of mountainside orchards that required less water—along with experiments in raising two crops per year along the Inland Sea. The shipping of timbers from Honshu's far regions to the temples of Nara illustrates how integrated Japan's provincial commerce was becoming. By the twelfth century, fewer adult villagers were dying of epidemics, as smallpox and measles generally became diseases of childhood alone. The true revolution in rural life, however, came in the 1300s and 1400s, when double cropping spread to a quarter of the nation's fields, and productivity soared.

The most surprising factor in all this was the emergence of villages. Through the Kamakura years, peasants typically had lived in simple dwellings scattered across a valley. Now, farmers and low-ranking samurai began coming together in hamlets to coordinate planting efforts and protect themselves from marauders. By the fifteenth century, communal building projects were producing fresh ridges between rice paddies, new ditches to bring water from nearby rivers, and lodgings for an increasingly prosperous peasant class. Villages began forming self-governing councils, called *sō*, which met in local shrines and oversaw a range of functions, from protecting residents against outsiders (including rapacious landowners) to coordinating the use of irrigation water and staging festivals to honor the local spirits. Villages also administered their own justice systems. The regulations of a village on Lake Biwa in 1492 revealed the typical approach. People who did not pay their taxes, they stated, would be evicted from their homes and denied fishing permits, and "mountain fields and collective possessions of the village that have been lent to them will be confiscated."[13] The ordinances of another village warned: "Do not give lodging to travelers." "Keeping dogs is forbidden."[14]

Many hamlets also joined together in *ikki* (leagues) or *sōkoku* (regional communes) to defend themselves against central authorities. Led by low-ranking warriors and prominent farmers, these groups used armed units and political tactics in the decades after the Ōnin Upheaval to secure their own autonomy and gain relief from debts and fees. Many wrote constitutions. They played a major role during the early 1500s in delaying the reemergence of central power. Ikkō, the largest league, brought together Pure Land Buddhists, peasants, and local samurai to create what its leaders called an "estate of Buddha," which for nearly a century after the 1470s controlled two entire provinces along the Sea of Japan coast.

With the emergence of villages came an end to serfdom, as peasants who had been indentured—or enslaved—to the *shōen* managers of earlier years now became small farmers, secured in their independence by the defensive village structure and the income from new crops such as dry-land vegetables and grains. That does not mean that life became easy for the former slaves, or for their hamlet neighbors. Natural disasters still produced famines; leprosy and epidemics devastated families; and domain or village taxes were heavy. The countryside was populated, too, by thieves, and tensions often arose between villagers and outcasts—people labeled *hinin* (nonpeople) or *eta* (filthy ones) because they engaged in despised occupations such as tanning, night soil collection, and public execution. Rural life nonetheless became more stable for most people during these centuries, and village products increased in number and variety.

Women also had a mixed experience. Most women found life more restrictive after Kamakura, but some, particularly those in the realm of religion, made strides. The standardization of marriage and of the wife's role as household manager made women more secure in the family, but brides now were required to move into the husband's household, as servant to the men and the mother-in-law—and that took away independence, rendering many wives little more than property. Women were hurt, too, by the rise of primogeniture, a system designed to keep family property intact by having the eldest male heir inherit everything. On the positive side, women still owned and managed property in some families, including the homes of Kyoto's shrunken nobility. Upper-class women also continued to produce high quality literary works, though without the renown of earlier times. And women became more fully integrated into popular Buddhist sects, often in leading roles. The nun Mugai Nyodai, for example, headed a network of convents in the Rinzai Zen tradition, insisting vigorously on the priest Dōgen's assertion that "learning the Law of Buddha and achieving release from illusion have nothing to do with whether one happens to be a man or a woman."[15]

Japan also experienced dynamic economic changes in the *sengoku* years. Towns and cities flourished, and by 1500 the country was dotted with rudimentary castle towns, alongside trade cities such as Sakai on the Inland Sea and Hakata in Kyushu. Most of these towns, with populations as large as 30,000, became both commercial and administrative hubs, alive with petty officials, construction workers, street performers, and merchants. In the countryside, the early Muromachi years saw the emergence of thrice-monthly local markets, offering everything from sesame seeds to barley and fish to knives—and in prosperous areas, silks from China and celadon bowls from Korea. By the era's end, many of the markets were open every sixth day. The country's roads now crisscrossed Honshu and Kyushu. Coins, imported from Ming China, largely replaced bartering as the unit of exchange, and money-lending made both temples and private families rich, with yearly interest rates as high as 300 percent.

Commerce was facilitated by the spread of *za* (guilds), typically made up of 10 to 100 firms in a given craft or specialty. The original purpose of the guilds was to secure a patron, perhaps a powerful temple or a *daimyō*, who would exempt them from taxes or tolls and give them a monopoly on their field, but the practical effect of their emergence was an increase in specialization and trade. The businesses organized by these guilds included nearly everything that was made and sold: oil, cotton, swords, fish, ink, clothing. Even actors' troupes formed *za*, to assure their monopoly on theaters in a particular region. The poet-priest Sōchō captured the guilds' spirit with his 1525 quip that those who enter "business for profit...never speak of gods or Buddhas" but "spend every waking moment thinking of making money." That, he said, "is how to get on in the world."[16]

This economic growth was accompanied by a significant expansion in international trade. Already in the late Heian years engagement with the continent had revived among private merchants, who traded everything from textiles and medicines to exotic birds and ceramics. By the Kamakura years, thirty-ton ships were making their way to eastern Japan, exchanging Japanese lumber for Chinese coins, cotton, silks, and luxury items. Then, in the Muromachi period, the Asian waters became truly international. The trade centered less on China now, thanks in part to the Ming dynasty's attempt to prohibit private trade, but the exchanges with Korea and southeast Asia grew. Okinawa became part of Japan's trade world, too, as merchants from the Ryūkyū Islands kingdom visited Japanese ports in search of swords and copper, and then provided ships for Japan's own exchanges with other countries. In 1458, the kingdom produced a bell with the inscription "By sailing our ships, we shall make Okinawa a bridge between countries."[17]

These interchanges led to a dramatically improved Japanese understanding of the nature of the Asian world. They also brought new wealth to a network of temples, *daimyō*, and merchant families, particularly in Kyushu and along the Inland Sea. Some sent out 250-ton ships now, carrying huge cargoes meant for exchange at high profits. A sunken fourteenth-century ship recovered off Korea in 1976 gives some sense of the scale of this trade. Apparently heading from China to Japan, the ninety-foot vessel was captained by a Japanese, had a multinational crew, and carried more than 18,000 ceramic objects, along with thousands of pounds of Chinese coins. Profits from such voyages could be immense, with Chinese silk selling in Japan for twenty times its original cost, for example, and Japanese swords marketed in China at a 500 percent profit.

This private trade was supplemented by the tribute trade that Yoshimitsu had initiated. On one level, the tribute embassies played a diplomatic role, undergirding the region's international relations system; on another level, they were trade missions. During Yoshimitsu's life, two ships a year went back and forth between China and Japan, carrying swords and gold to be exchanged for coins and textiles. The official embassies were more sporadic after his death, as *daimyō* and temples gained increasing control of the tribute trade, but missions continued until the mid-1500s. A flourishing trade also developed with Korea, as the kings of the Choson dynasty signed agreements with the *bakufu* and various *daimyō*, as well as with the Sō family on Tsushima Island. The Japanese were particularly eager to secure Korean cotton (nearly six million yards were purchased in 1486) and full sets of the Buddhist scriptures, which had been printed in Korea but not in Japan. Over the 1400s, they prided themselves on being able to secure forty-three complete sets of the Buddhist canon.

Pirates engaged in a less savory but no less extensive brand of trade. Officials had long struggled to control the brigands who plundered ships (sometimes at the behest of Japanese temples), but the problem remained manageable until the mid-1300s, when piracy soared. By the late 1370s, Japanese pirates were making more than forty yearly raids along the Korean coasts, with as many as 400 ships, 3,000 men, and a bevy of horses in a raiding party. Sometimes they captured hostages for labor back in Japan. Other times they seized shipments of rice that were being sent to the capital as tax payments. The Korean kings protested, and so did the Chinese after coming under heavy attack in the late 1300s; but the Muromachi officials were powerless to suppress them. Yongle, the frustrated Ming emperor, commented: "Ships could not readily reach them, nor could spears or arrows readily touch them.

We could not move them by bestowing benefits on them; nor could we awe them by pressing them with our might."[18]

No area of life remained immune to the vast changes in society—not even religion, which took on a more popular tone during this era, even as Buddhist priests pioneered new approaches to the arts. As in earlier times, the established organizations remained powerful and affluent, equally active in the worlds of commerce, politics, and religion, but the greatest changes, particularly in the Kamakura period, came with the impressive expansion of the populist Buddhist branches, particularly the Pure Land movements and the exclusivist Nichiren sect. All of these proclaimed the Buddhist idea of *mappō* (end of the law), which held that humankind had entered its last days. They also maintained that faith alone—either in the Buddha Amida or in Buddhism's central scripture, the Lotus Sutra—would bring people enlightenment. And they insisted that salvation was available to *all* people: poor and rich, female and male.

These sects grew in part because they were propagated by charismatic, controversial leaders. Pure Land founder Hōnen, who said people should perpetually recite the praise-to-Amida chant (*nembutsu*), offended the establishment with his appeal to the masses and was banished as an old man to the island of Shikoku. His spiritual heir, Shinran, founder of the True Pure Land sect, went even further, arguing that a single recitation of the *nembutsu* was sufficient for rebirth in the Pure Land. "If a good man can attain salvation," he said, "even more so a wicked man"—so all-encompassing was the power of Amida's compassion.[19] The first Buddhist priest to marry publicly, he, too, was exiled. Nichiren's style was different. While agreeing that salvation was for everyone, he propounded an exclusivist theology, railing against other religious and secular authorities and arguing that salvation was available only through belief in the Lotus Sutra. He scoffed that "the *nembutsu* leads to hell" and called for Pure Land temples to "be burned to the ground and their priests beheaded."[20] He, too, was exiled—twice. All three men attracted great numbers of followers.

Zen, another sect that emerged in Kamakura, reached full flower in the Muromachi years, when its Rinzai branch established some 300 monasteries. Nurtured by priests who had studied in China, Zen maintained Buddhism's more traditional emphasis on the centrality of temples and was more intellectual than the Amida sects, maintaining that enlightenment was found within one's self, through meditation and discipline. As the Zen pioneer Dōgen expressed it: "Enlightenment is something like the reflection of the moon in water.... Though the light of the moon is vast and immense, it finds a home in water only a foot long and an inch wide."[21] The reason Zen prospered lay less in its intellectualism, which many warriors found obscure, than in its ties to the samurai establishment. Its Chinese orientation appealed to *bakufu* officials, and the expertise of monks who had studied on the continent was useful in diplomacy and trade. Its emphasis on austere arts such as ink painting and calligraphy also held great appeal.

Nowhere was the spreading impact of Buddhism more apparent than in medieval art and literature. Buddhist ideas such as evanescence and nonattachment pervaded nearly all Kamakura writings. The *Tales of the Heike*, for example, which chronicled the fall of the Taira family, begins: "The sound of the bell of Jetavana echoes the impermanence of all things.... They who flourish must be brought low."[22] Kamo Chōmei's *Account of My Hut* relates a priest's search for solace in a ten-foot-square mountainside cottage after becoming disillusioned by the troubles of the world. "I rejoice in the absence of grief," he says. He loves his tiny hut, yet at the end he sighs: "My attachment to its solitude may also be a hindrance to salvation."[23] These stories have a heaviness, a consciousness of conflict, that is not present in the courtly Heian writings.

Similar themes suffused Muromachi literature. *Essays in Idleness*, a miscellany of reflections reminiscent of the *Pillow Book*, brims with witty yet melancholy comments: on life's brevity, on the foolishness of heavy drinking, on the way we forget those who have died. The representative works of this period are the Nō drama scripts, which use spare prose to narrate tales of dead warriors, priests, and officials who have come back as ghosts, often to meet a lover or to repair some damage. The opening lines of the play *Atsumori* are typical. Kumagai, the warrior who took the head of the young flute player, proclaims: "Life is a lying dream, he only wakes who casts the world aside." The play ends with Atsumori's ghost beseeching Kumagai (now a priest): "Pray for me again, oh pray for me again."[24] Not all Muromachi literature is dark. Short, witty *kyōgen* plays were presented during the interludes between Nō performances, and traveling storytellers recounted tales that were as entertaining as they were didactic. Most of the major works, however, reflect the Buddhist preoccupation with impermanence, reinforced by the somber times in which they were written.

Zen's greatest influence may have been in the visual sphere, where its emphasis on meditation and discipline inspired many of Japan's most innovative art forms. Priests like Sesshū and Shūbun gave us the era's angular mountain-filled landscapes, along with its richly suggestive

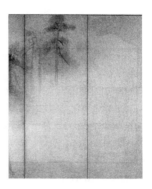

Hasegawa Tōhaku was famed for ink paintings such as the six-panel Pine Trees, *done late in the sixteenth century. The trees illustrate the impact of Zen Buddhism on medieval Japanese painters, who sought to convey complex natural scenes with ink alone, employing a minimum number of brush strokes. Shading was used to suggest a forest in the mists—or perhaps in a snowstorm.* TNM Image Archives.

brush paintings. Monks also gave us the spare arts of flower arrangement, calligraphy, tea-bowl pottery, and the *tatami*-mat flooring of elite Muromachi homes. The era's visual culture was not devoid of the colorful or the gaudy; witness the gold plating of Yoshimitsu's Kinkakuji or the colorful screen paintings of the late Muromachi Kanō school. But the dominating tone was rustic simplicity.

Gardening and the tea ceremony illustrate the Zen influence with particular force. The Japanese had built gardens for centuries, but Muromachi priests and craftsmen took them in radical directions. The purpose of the Zen viewing garden was to encourage tranquility by symbolizing the natural world in a small space. To that end, elites of the 1400s commissioned commoners, known as "dry riverbed people" (for the place of their poor forebears' dwellings), to design areas that used simple objects to invoke a bigger universe: ragged rocks to suggest a waterfall, grouped pebbles a flowing stream. The most famous Muromachi garden remaining today is the rock garden of Kyoto's Ryōanji temple, a space that contains nothing but fifteen stones in a rectangle of raked sand, surrounded by clay walls and tall conifers. These gardens also served, on many occasions, as a setting for the tea ceremony, which some see as Japan's quintessential art. Tea drinking had been popular since the twelfth century, and in the 1300s rich families held lavish tea-tasting parties. Now, in the violent *sengoku* years, this pursuit was turned into a contemplative art: a few people, sitting on the floor of a bare hut, drinking the bitter liquid in three and a half sips, then eating a small sweet, as the breeze outside evokes life's vicissitudes. Life's deepest meaning, Zen says, is found in the ordinary; so is the soul of art.

Taken as a whole, the medieval years gave birth to a dramatic evolution in the nature of Japanese life, stimulated by the rise of the warrior class and the innovations of merchants, villagers, and priests. To be sure, the political system underwent highly important changes: from a two-headed military/civilian government in the 1200s through an increasingly weak center under Ashikaga leadership, to a collapse of the central order after the Ōnin Upheaval. At least as important were the cultural and social changes that derived only part of their force from the old systems. Commerce flourished along new transportation routes and in new cities. Influences and income from the continent provided both ideas and wealth. Peasants formed villages and markets. Religion became the possession of the weak as well as the mighty. And the arts took radically new forms. People who limit their vision to central institutions find much that is frustrating in medieval Japan; those who focus on the countryside see an era rich in innovation and full of energy.

CHAPTER 4

Peace—And Its Benefits (1550–1850)

On an April day in 1771, the physician Sugita Genpaku watched, rapt, while an old man of the outcast class dissected the corpse of a criminal known as Old Mother Green Tea. Days before, Sugita had acquired two Dutch anatomy books filled with sketches of human organs that "looked so different from the pictures in the Chinese anatomical books" that he decided he had to see the inside of a body for himself. "Comparing the things we saw with the pictures in the Dutch book," he said, "we were amazed at their perfect agreement."[1] He and a friend decided to translate one of the books, *Ontleedkundige Tafelen* (Anatomical tables), into Japanese, even though they did not know Dutch, an act that, in its turn, fed a growing intellectual movement known as Dutch studies.

Sugita's discovery hints at the many ways Japan had changed since the Tokugawa family had assumed the reins of government in 1600. The presence of the Dutch books shows that Japan had become part of a broader world, while the ignorance of anatomy suggests a society closed to many Western influences. The doctor's determination to get at the truth typifies the passion for knowledge that drove Japan's intellectuals, whereas his later difficulties in getting the translation published illustrate the government's determination to control ideas. The outcast origins of the dissector reveal a society in which classes and social groups were defined quite strictly, even as peoples intermingled in wholly new ways. The fact that Sugita hailed from the Japan Sea regions yet grew up in the capital city shows how interconnected the country had become. The Tokugawa system brought Japan 250 years of peace; it also gave it two centuries of commercial and intellectual energy, along with a new way of seeing the world—and the most comprehensive government system the country had known. It was in these years that Japan, for the first time, came close to being a true national unit.

The backdrop for this era was a half-century of intensified warfare, leading toward reunification. By the mid–sixteenth century, several regional coalitions of *daimyō* had emerged from the *sengoku* period's political chaos, and after the 1560s, two *daimyō* and a foot soldier's son—known to history as the "three unifiers"—successively took control of ever-wider regions, until by 1600 Japan had become a single political domain. The first of the three was a short man named Oda Nobunaga who lived by the slogan "Rule by force." He drove the last Ashikaga shogun from Kyoto in 1573, destroyed the powerful Tendai Buddhist temples on Mount Hiei and the Ikkō league on the Japan Sea by slaughtering thousands of their priests and defenders, constructed an ostentatious castle north of Kyoto, and took control of most of central and western Honshu. In 1582, he was assassinated by one of his own lieutenants as he headed off toward new conquests in the west, whereupon the foot soldier's son Toyotomi Hideyoshi, now a general, took control of the Oda forces.

Toyotomi, whom Oda nicknamed "Monkey," took less than a decade to complete Japan's unification, sending armies of up to 200,000 against rivals in Kyushu, Shikoku, and finally Sendai far to the north. Still not satisfied with his accomplishments, he then sent troops to Korea in 1592 and again in 1597—determined to become ruler of the East Asian world. The Korean adventures were disastrous in every respect: undermining China's Ming dynasty, which overspent itself in defending Korea, wreaking havoc within Korea, and humiliating Hideyoshi himself. More successful were his administrative initiatives at home, which laid the foundation for centuries of stable rule. He used land surveys and rice production records to create a tax system rooted in reliable data about who lived where and what they produced. He seized control of the country's gold and silver mines and promoted foreign trade. In an effort to get control of the military, he denied farmers the right "to possess long swords, short swords, bows, spears, muskets, or any other form of weapon,"[2] and then melted down their confiscated weapons to make temple bells and other implements. He also patronized the arts, particularly the tea ceremony. The complexity of the man—militarist, megalomaniac, charmer, art lover, astute administrator—is symbolized by the two teahouses he maintained, one a rustic hut that evoked the simplicity of Zen, the other an ostentatious structure gilded inside and out.

The Korean fiasco was not the only challenge to Hideyoshi's long-term ambitions; another lay in his inability to produce a strong heir. When he died in 1598, his only potential successor was a five-year-old son. As a result, his ally-turned-rival Tokugawa Ieyasu wrested power from the Toyotomi family two years later, and established a new regime 300 miles to the east in Edo, where Tokyo sits today. A popular children's story has it that if a canary had refused to sing, Oda would have crushed it; Toyotomi would have persuaded it to sing; and Tokugawa would simply have waited it out. That, as it turned out, was the strategy that succeeded. It was not, however, a strategy designed to give confidence in Tokugawa's ability to govern well. Japan, after all, faced massive challenges in 1600. It still was mired in the mental habits of war. Its imperial institution was in shambles. There were few models for countrywide administration.

And there was a relatively new threat, which would profoundly influence the way the Tokugawa governed: hundreds of gun- and Bible-bearing Westerners who had come to make a profit and save souls. The first Europeans had reached Japan by accident in 1543, shipwrecked on Tanegashima, an island off southern Kyushu. Over the rest of the sixteenth century, traders and missionaries came in significant numbers, opening windows to the non-Asian world, enriching coastal *daimyō* through trade, and converting perhaps 300,000 Japanese to Christianity. Most Europeans were impressed by the Japanese, echoing the Jesuit pioneer Francis Xavier, who pronounced them "the best who have yet been discovered," a people of "very good manners, good in general and not malicious."[3] The response of most Japanese is reflected in the label they gave the newcomers: southern barbarians. While Oda used their muskets and coastal *daimyō* employed their ships to trade with Southeast Asians and Chinese, the Europeans' politics and religion worried them. Hideyoshi, for his part, turned on the Westerners in 1587, despite his desire for trade, and ordered all foreign Christians to leave the country, fearful about their territorial ambitions. He never enforced the order, but several years later he had twenty-six Christians (including six European priests) crucified, after hearing rumors that Spanish priests often prepared an area for conquest. Ieyasu harbored similar suspicions and acted forcefully, brutally at times, to keep the foreign threat under control.

Despite the many threats, the Tokugawa succeeded in establishing a stable state. The contrast between their world and that of the *sengoku* years was great. Two and a half centuries of peace replaced endemic warfare. The administrative capital shifted to the Tokugawa home base of Edo. Warring *daimyō* domains gave way to an intricate structure that divided power between the center and the peripheries. Whereas Japan excluded foreigners more systematically than ever before, it became more fully integrated into the global world. These changes were more evolutionary than revolutionary, because Ieyasu's goal was to keep rivals in check rather than to eradicate enemies or secure absolute power over the domains of individual *daimyō*. Nevertheless, by the mid-1600s he and his successors had created the most all-encompassing administrative structure Japan had ever known, a structure that allowed roughly 250 domains (called *han* after the early 1700s) to coexist peacefully for a quarter of a millennium, while commerce and culture developed dramatically.

The first goal of the Tokugawa government was to maintain peace. More interested in order than innovation, Ieyasu and his followers showed little interest in developing nationwide tax, military, or judicial systems but endeavored instead to ensure their own ascendancy within a stable, relatively decentralized system. To that end, they left the emperors on the throne in Kyoto, assuring their material well-being while insisting that Kyoto follow the Tokugawa will. They retained the traditional religious institutions but turned temples into census-taking branches of the government. And they devised an administrative structure that used old names—shogun and *bakufu*—to invoke an aura of antiquity and legitimacy yet created new mechanisms designed to give each *daimyō* autonomy in his own domain while Edo administered Tokugawa lands and handled regime-wide duties such as the supervision of international relations and the maintenance of highways, mines, and mints.

Scholars call the system *bakuhan* because of the balance it maintained between the Edo *bakufu* and the regional *han*. The Tokugawa retained the right to eradicate or relocate *daimyō*, but they never considered wiping out their main rivals, and after an initial period of reorganization and consolidation, they left most domains intact. Each *han* was permitted to maintain its own military and tax systems and to make its own laws, as long as it followed certain rules, which included securing Edo's permission for *daimyō* family marriages and providing monetary and labor support for Edo projects such as palace construction and flood prevention. The result was that regional Japan experienced significant growth and diversity, while Ieyasu's descendants got the stability they sought.

The most effective—and interesting—means of assuring *daimyō* cooperation was the *sankin kōtai* or alternate attendance system, which by 1635 required lords to leave their wives and children in Edo permanently, as hostages, and to spend alternating periods (usually a year) there themselves, assisting the shogun. This system was effective as a control technique, keeping lords away from their *han* half the time and burdening them with the expenses of maintaining large residential compounds in Edo and making regular trips with hundreds of retainers to and from the capital. Its unanticipated impact in stimulating national

Osaka castle, a modern reconstruction of one of the massive, multistoried daimyō
*structures that served as headquarters of each domain in the Tokugawa years
(1600–1868). These castles served as living quarters and administrative centers
for the* daimyō, *typically housing hundreds of family members and servants.
Surrounded by one or more moats, set on a base of hewn stone, and topped by
white plastered walls and tile roofs, the castles were intended as much to show the
lord's strength as to provide defense.* Photo by Chris McCooey.

development was equally important. The ceaseless travel of hundreds of *daimyō* contingents required a more extensive nationwide network than ever of well-maintained highways and towns for lodging, eating, and entertainment. The intermingling of the *han* elites in Edo, where they competed for prestige and status, created nationwide fashions and tastes. The fact that nearly all *daimyō* grew up in Edo, as part of the hostage system, intensified the growing sense of a common culture.

That sense was also encouraged by the *bakufu*'s efforts to create a unified ideology and to handle foreign affairs at the national level. The regime used religion as a support for the state from the first, enshrining Ieyasu as a Buddhist avatar at the huge Shintō shrines in Nikkō. As the generations passed, the focus shifted to Neo-Confucianism, a system barely known in Japan until the late 1500s. Under a series of state advisors, including the brilliant Confucian thinker Ogyū Sorai early in the 1700s, the Tokugawa came to be seen as the rightful guardians of the "heavenly way," legitimized by their ability to discern and implement the principles necessary for keeping society orderly. "One's first concern," Ogyū wrote, "should be Humane Government." He said, "The lord of a province should regard his warriors and the general population as a family that has been given him by Heaven, a family that he cannot abandon." The duty of a subject, he added, was loyalty: "serving one's lord and nurturing and putting him at ease."[4] At the practical level, this ideology divided society into four descending classes or status groups—samurai, farmers, craftsmen, and merchants, in that order—and gave expression to a new term, *bushidō*, which maintained that the "way of the warrior" was to lead society and live by a rigorous ethical code.

In foreign relations, the regime had two goals: security and prosperity. To ensure the latter, *bakufu* officials established Nagasaki as a center for trade with China and Europe, and they fostered relations with Korea and the Ryūkyū islands through the *daimyō* of Tsushima Island and the southern domain of Satsuma, respectively. Both Korea and the Ryūkyūs sent large missions to Edo to celebrate major events such as the accession of a new shogun, with the Korean delegations typically numbering more than 400 members. On occasion, the Tokugawa also used force, particularly to assure the cooperation of the Ryūkyū islanders and the indigenous people of Hokkaido in the north, the Ainu. All of this resulted in lively trade exchanges in the 1600s, with silver and gold flowing out and silks flowing in. As the century neared an end, however, officials began focusing more on security and less on profit, with the result that trade declined after 1700.

Security measures were most obvious in Nagasaki. Partly to avoid being placed in a subordinate position in Asia's China-centered order and partly to prevent Western aggression, the *bakufu* issued a series of regulations that, by the 1630s, limited the Chinese to a community of 2,000 traders in a sector of Nagasaki and restricted Western trade to a man-made island in Nagasaki harbor called Dejima. The main target of these rules was Christianity, which was proscribed. Under Ieyasu's grandson, Iemitsu, as many as 5,000 Christians were executed, sometimes by crucifixion. In 1635, a sweeping edict proclaimed, "No Japanese is permitted to go abroad" and "If any Japanese returns from overseas after residing there, he must be put to death."[5] An unsuccessful uprising two years later by 25,000 commoners carrying Christian banners on Kyushu's Shimabara peninsula confirmed Tokugawa security fears and spurred still harsher policies. By 1641, the Spaniards and Portuguese had been banned and the British had stopped coming, leaving the Dutch as the only Europeans in Japan.

Even the Dutch were regulated vigorously—restricted to tiny Dejima, where they were secluded from ordinary Japanese. Visited by just three trading ships a year on average, they led dreary lives. Englebert Kaempfer, a Dejima physician in the early 1690s, likened the island's buildings to goat-pens and said its inhabitants were treated "not like honest men but like criminals, traitors, spies, prisoners, or, to say the least, as...hostages of the shogun, as the locals always (thoughtfully) call us."[6] Profits kept the traders coming, however, and the information about Europe that they provided on annual visits to Edo persuaded officials that the system should be maintained. In other words, the Dutch and Chinese gave the *bakufu* exactly what it desired at the end of the 1600s: prosperity and knowledge, within a stable trading system.

The regime's dominance was less pronounced on the domestic level, where it did a better job of fostering security than of controlling national life. As the centuries unfolded, development initiative was taken increasingly by the villages, towns, and domains. Although *bakufu* policies remained important to the end of the era, the country's most dynamic changes were inspired by people outside the capital, the commoners and elites in far-flung domains who generated economic, literary, and cultural transformations that could not have been predicted in 1600. These changes were crucial in moving Japan toward nationhood.

The 1600s saw remarkable gains in nearly every area of society, and though the momentum slowed after that, growth in many regions continued into the 1800s. Population, for example, soared in the seventeenth century, from 12 million to perhaps 25 million. Land planted in rice doubled. Living standards improved for all classes (though not for all individuals), providing bigger homes, better foods, more comfortable clothes, and greater longevity. The country's transportation system advanced: sign-dotted highways like the Edo-to-Kyoto Tōkaidō were crowded with pilgrim groups traveling to shrines, villagers off to hot springs, peddlers carrying their wares, and *daimyō* processions heading to and from the capital, alongside begging nuns and pickpockets. The roadways were "as crowded as the streets of a populous European city," Kaempfer said, because "the Japanese travel more often than other people."[7] Moreover, travel had become safer than in the medieval years, as one eighteenth-century samurai noted: "Wherever I go [the inhabitants], from lords and officials to poor fishermen and woodcutters, treat me politely, and I have been able to wander with ease."[8]

The *han* gave birth to many of the era's most significant changes. Autonomy allowed each domain to develop its own distinctive commercial and administrative practices, thereby spurring both economic growth and regional differences. Interdomain trade created national commercial networks and credit systems, as well as a cash economy, but each domain created its own currency. When labor grew scarce, one domain might encourage outsiders to immigrate, while another subsidized its own households to keep them from leaving. When hard times hit, one *han* encouraged samurai wives to go into silk weaving; another suggested that warriors become farmers—both deviations from the neo-Confucian ethos. Even the era's terminology suggested local independence: domains often referred to themselves not as *han* but as *kuni* (countries). When the lord of Yonezawa in the far north asserted that he thought "of the entire country [*kuni*] as one family,"[9] he meant not Japan but his *han*.

A vivid illustration of the changes that swept regional Japan came in the rapid growth of villages and cities, with small localities undergoing even more sustained transformation than the cities. Villagers made up some 80 percent of Tokugawa Japan's population. They flooded the rice paddies in the spring, transplanted seedlings into the muddy fields, harvested the grain in autumn, and then paid taxes and rents from their harvest. Other villagers fished the coasts, mined the mountains, and fed mulberry leaves to silkworms. They demonstrated the two sides of Tokugawa development: continuing poverty for many, set against impressive growth for increasing numbers of rural residents.

The difficult side of village life was everywhere apparent. A quick reading of early Edo village regulations suggests how restricted—and grim—village life could be: "*sake* must not be brewed in villages"; "no design is permitted" in peasant clothing; "bean-jam buns, bean curds and the like may not be traded."[10] And economic realities often turned grimness to darkness. Poverty was everywhere. Famines ravaged wide areas, as did epidemics of smallpox and syphilis. Taxes wore people down. And pollution took a toll in mining regions. In the words of a 1745 peasant petition in Sachiu village of the northeast: "Polluted water reaches the fields, and farmers suffer the extreme inconvenience of having crops that do not ripen. When mining was conducted in this location previously, rice fields...all became barren."[11]

Problems also sprang from a status system that sometimes provoked conflicts between villagers and the outcast groups of leather-workers, jailhouse employees, and undertakers who frequently lived nearby. While the *eta* and *hinin* experienced a great deal of autonomy within their own group structures, Tokugawa rules made the separation between commoners and outcasts more rigid than in earlier centuries. They required that *eta* and *hinin* live in their own spaces, outside the farming villages, and forbade them from entering commoners' homes, socializing with them, or dressing like them. That did not keep some outcastes from doing well financially, since many of their functions were in high demand. But it exacerbated tensions between groups and intensified the stigma that went with outsider status.

More surprising—and even more remarkable—was the dynamic side of Tokugawa village life. Regulations notwithstanding, most villagers could conduct life as they pleased, as long as they paid their taxes and avoided calling attention to themselves. As one village headman put it: "So long as he can get to his paddies and fields to work, he can make his living without hardship. The only one who can...say whatever he pleases is the peasant."[12] Having helped to fuel the economy in the 1600s, the villages kept growing in the 1700s, after the cities lost their momentum. One evidence of this lies in the villages' increased productivity. Although the amount of arable land stayed relatively constant in the 1700s, output continued to rise, thanks to better farming techniques. Crop varieties expanded as farmers supplemented rice with corn, sweet potatoes, cotton, silk, sugar, and tobacco. Many villages developed nonagricultural businesses, too. The people of mountainous Shimoina in Nagano, for example, prospered from their packhorse transportation and wood products. The fishermen of Hokkaido sold herring-meal fertilizer for cotton fields.

Indeed, the dominant rural trait of this increasingly industrial era may have been the commercial spirit, as farmers everywhere read treatises on agricultural techniques, worked to create economies of scale, and borrowed money to secure seed grain and to live better. One indignant moralist said early in the 1800s: "The most lamentable abuse of the present day among the peasants is that those who have become wealthy forget their status and live luxuriously like city aristocrats."[13] One wonders if he also was angry that bathing and the regular washing of clothes had become widespread. Or that commoners in small towns now got to watch touring sumo wrestlers?

Growth in the cities may not have been as sustained, but was impressive, too, particularly in the early Tokugawa period. During the 1600s, cities proliferated across the country, mainly as a result of the new political structure. Each domain had its castle town, often with a population of more than 10,000, and villages expanded into towns along the major highways, partly to service the *sankin kōtai* processions. Major centers such as Osaka (the commercial hub) and Kyoto (the manufacturing center) grew dramatically in the seventeenth century, with populations reaching 375,000 in Kyoto and 500,000 in Osaka by the early 1700s. The most spectacular expansion came in Edo, the bay-side swampland Ieyasu chose as his administrative center. Within decades, its diverse sections had been crisscrossed by canals, linked by bridges, bedecked with *daimyō* quarters—and filled with hundreds of thousands of samurai and commoners, come to work for the *bakufu*. By the 1700s, Edo's population numbered more than a million, making it the world's largest city. According to one estimate, towns and cities, which made up about 1 percent of Japan's population in 1600, constituted 15 percent in the early 1700s.[14]

Samurai made up a significant portion of most cities' populations, even though they constituted only 7 percent of Japan's people overall. In theory, these warriors lived off government stipends in return for administering public life. In reality, there were not enough government jobs for them, and their official incomes generally were meager. As a result, many had to look elsewhere for money. Some became physicians; some started schools; some taught swordsmanship; many engaged in work considered beneath their class; most borrowed money. Poverty was common. Katsu Kokichi, an Edo samurai of fairly distinguished lineage, wrote a memoir about his life as a ne'er-do-well in the early 1800s. At age twenty-one, he wrote, he was "penniless. I had no choice but to sell my everyday sword....I had only the clothes on my back. To take my mind off my woes, I went to the Yoshiwara" pleasure quarters.[15] In some regions, a full 70 percent of these warriors put food on the table by means of unorthodox money-making schemes—everything from making dolls to hiring out their daughters as servants. And many frequented the gambling halls that spread across the country in the 1700s.

Much of the samurai spending went into the coffers of the *chōnin*, or townsmen classes, who provided the bulk of the cities' energy. Technically, the term *chōnin* denoted all nonsamurai urbanites, at least half of whom were the workers who built the houses, carried away the night soil, fought the fires, and provided the transportation that kept urban life functioning. In common use, however, the term referred to the merchants and craftsmen who were free from taxation and from ideological constraints on profit-making—and thus able to exploit every city dweller's needs and desires. While most *chōnin* were poor, many were entrepreneurs. In Osaka, they created the world's first commodity futures market and facilitated a nationwide rice trade. In Kyoto, they handled the shogun's finances and produced Japan's best textiles. In Edo, they designed *daimyō* residences, ran factories, and worked for the samurai. In castle towns, they exchanged goods between city and countryside. And everywhere, firms with names like Mitsui and Noda Shōyu (later Kikkoman) operated soy sauce factories, invented mining technologies, brewed sake, and operated fish markets and entertainment quarters. They also sold Buddhist relics, ran bathhouses, organized specialized trade guilds, and generally turned Japan's cities into profit-making engines.

The *chōnin* also inspired a noticeable leveling of society, status distinctions notwithstanding. No one could have doubted that some kind of social transformation was afoot when walking through the evening and morning marketplaces around Osaka's and Edo's bridges, thronged by shoppers from all strata, out to sample everything from radishes to candy, from street entertainment to smoked herring—or when observing the colorful tattoos sported by shoppers from nearly all classes except the samurai after the early 1800s. One of the most important engines of this leveling was an explosion in printing, mostly wood block but also moveable type, in the early Tokugawa decades. The era saw a flood of published works: travel guides, farmers' manuals, sermon collections, joke books, and one-page broadsides, called *kawaraban*, that gave Japan its first taste of journalism, with sensational stories about castle fires or temple sex scandals—all for a profit, of course. An average of 3,000 published works a year bound people together in an intellectual community rendered possible by printing.

Social leveling was stimulated, too, by the spread of schools. Until 1600, education had been limited to the elite. Now, the expansion of commerce and printing, along with a more expansive political system, made the benefits of learning obvious everywhere and prompted the widespread creation of schools: private schools run by intellectuals, official *han* and *bakufu* institutions, and thousands of local academies run by priests, husband-and-wife teams, or underemployed samurai. Teachers, many of whom were women and nearly half of whom were commoners, were often paid in gifts rather than cash, and instruction involved tedious hours of writing from copybooks. By the early 1800s, roughly 40 percent of Japan's males and 10 percent of its females had achieved literacy—a remarkable figure for the nineteenth-century world. The impact of these schools on social attitudes is apparent in an 1843 *bakufu* order: "Teachers who run schools both within the city of Edo and without should instruct children enthusiastically and treat them equally. Everyone—boys and girls, high and low—should be able to read and write appropriate to their station."[16] Class and status still mattered, but less than they once had.

Most people went to school to learn to do accounts or read instructions. The schools, however, also supported a lively intellectual life among *chōnin* and samurai elites. Indeed, by the end of the second Tokugawa century, the system had produced great numbers of scholars and commentators who engaged in lively exchanges about the direction of national life. There were Confucian scholars who looked to China for models. There were *kokugaku* (national learning) advocates who sought direction in Japan's own past, merchant ethicists who lauded hard work, and, increasingly, students of "Dutch learning," a sobriquet for anything Western. The last group remained small in number until the late eighteenth century because of the ban on the study of anything related to Christianity, but after that works such as Sugita's Dutch anatomy gained increasing attention even from officials.

Then there were the arts, the sphere on which the *chōnin* put their most colorful stamp. Within the governing class and among families who cared about pedigree, the prestigious arts, called *ga*, still thrived, perpetuating traditional forms such as Nō theater and the tea ceremony. But it was the entertainment pursuits of the townsman, activities the samurai labeled *zoku* (coarse), that gave theater, literature, and the visual arts their greatest energy, leveling urban culture almost as much as education did.

The cities' entertainment centers, or pleasure quarters, spawned many of the *zoku* artistic developments. By the late 1600s, each major city boasted an area called the *ukiyo* or "floating world," where men (and more than a few women) from all classes sought relief from the strictures of daily life. At the heart of these quarters—Shinmachi in

Osaka, Shimabara in Kyoto, Yoshiwara in Edo—was an assortment of bathhouses, theaters, teahouses, and brothels offering pleasures of every sort. The key figures were the female entertainers, known after the mid-1700s as *geisha*, who danced, sang, and made conversation with male visitors. *Oiran*, or courtesans, also were important to each entertainment district, prompting the travel writer Hiraga Gennai to comment in the 1760s: "The lanterns burned brighter than daylight, illuminating the sumptuously bedecked courtesans as they sat before tobacco trays cooly smoking, or writing letters. Wayward strands of black hair lay quaintly against their white collars....Women such as this could not be of this world."[17]

From the *ukiyo* quarters came a multifaceted set of art and literary forms. On the stage, the lively spectacles and intricate plots of kabuki attracted attendees from all classes, even though samurai attendance was theoretically forbidden. Kabuki acting, which had originated in provocative dances by women along Kyoto's Kamo River in the late 1500s, was restricted to adult males after the 1650s, and eventually the *onnagata*, or female impersonators, were among its most popular figures. Fantasy also gave *bunraku* (puppet theater) much of its allure, with men in black manipulating realistic puppets in full view of the audience. Like kabuki, *bunraku* attracted adults from all walks of life, and its greatest playwright, Chikamatsu Monzaemon, produced many literary masterpieces, including *Love Suicide at Sonezaki*, in which a clerk and a prostitute die together rather than accept prohibitions on cross-class marriage. The era's major visual innovation, the woodblock print, derived both its name and its initial content from the *ukiyo*. Known as *ukiyo-e* or "floating world pictures," the first of these prints were stylized portraits of leading courtesans in the entertainment world; later woodblocks depicted broader subjects such as commoner life and landscapes. Although they were not respected as genuine art at the time, they were immensely popular, displayed on the walls of huts and mansions alike.

The era's most highly regarded literature came from *chōnin* society, too. While officials may have praised Buddhist sermons and Confucian discourses, the denizens of the pleasure quarters turned out the masterpieces, bringing new realism to fiction and boasting sales large enough to allow writers, for the first time, to earn a living from their brushes. The era's leading novelist was the Osaka native Ihara Saikaku, who first won renown for poetry, then produced more than twenty books about lovers, samurai, and merchants. His first famous work, *A Man Who Chose Love*, recounted the amorous experiences of a man who

For two years (1794–95), the popular woodblock artist Sharaku produced numerous exaggerated portraits of kabuki actors, such as this one of Ōtani Oniji II, and then he mysteriously disappeared from public life—a fact that gave him a special mystique and increased his popularity among art lovers. The major dramatic form of the Tokugawa years, kabuki was performed only by male actors, many of whom became nationwide celebrities. TNM Image Archives.

retired at age sixty to an island inhabited only by women. Another, *Five Women Who Chose Love*, described the passionate affairs of women in respectable society, while a third portrayed homosexual attraction. His wittiest novel was probably *The Eternal Storehouse of Japan*, a description of merchants making money. In one episode, several visitors sit in wealthy Fuji-ichi's home speculating on what food is being prepared in the kitchen. After a discourse on frugality, Fuji-ichi concludes: "It is high time that refreshments were served. But not to provide refreshments is one way of becoming a millionaire. The noise of the mortar which you heard...was the pounding of starch for the covers of the Account Book."[18]

Saikaku's Genroku-period contemporary, Matsuo Bashō, also exemplified the era's social leveling. His father was a samurai, but of lowly status, barely able to make a living teaching and possibly farming. Bashō's great contribution was to poetry and travel writing. Revered as history's greatest writer of the three-line haiku form, he is best known for his "frog verse":

> The old pond
> A frog jumps in—
> A sound of splashing.

The popularity of haiku among peoples across the land is illustrated in a tale from one of his trips, when he reputedly happened on a group of villagers composing poems beneath a full moon. Posing as a pilgrim priest, he first declined when asked to compose something, then finally responded:

> 'Twas the new moon
> Since then I waited—
> And lo! tonight!

The farmers gasped when they learned that their visitor was Bashō, "whose fragrant name was known to all the world."[19] The next centuries would produce a plethora of popular haiku poets, along with emulators of Saikaku's witty, earthy fiction style.

For all of the dynamism of the first two Tokugawa centuries, a sense of national crisis dominated public discussions as the 1800s approached. *Bakufu* leadership had failed to keep up with social changes, and officials seemed adrift; economic development had stagnated, particularly in the urban sphere, and writers had begun to invoke the impending doom suggested by the Chinese concept of *naiyū gaikan*—"troubles within, dangers without." On the domestic side, mounting financial difficulties

BRADFORD WG LIBRARY
100 HOLLAND COURT, BOX 130
BRADFORD, ONT. L3Z 2A7

were cited frequently as the cause of the problems. Official admonitions about frugality notwithstanding, by the early 1800s the shogun's government was taking in 500,000 fewer gold coins, called *ryō*, than it was spending each year. Some domains did better than the Tokugawa, but most of them struggled, too; the relatively affluent Chōshū *han*, for example, owed *all* of its tax revenues in 1840 to merchants from whom it had taken out loans. Administrators resorted to a raft of income-producing measures: reducing the metal content of coins, forcing merchants to loan them money, cutting samurai stipends—and occasionally carrying out drastic reform programs, as in the cost-cutting administration of the senior *bakufu* councillor Mizuno Tadakuni early in the 1840s. But the fiscal crises only worsened as time passed.

The sense of domestic crisis was compounded by a rise in commoner protests after the 1780s, provoked sometimes by famines, sometimes by taxes, and often by corrupt or heavy-handed officials. One of the most destructive uprisings was led by the idealistic Osaka constable Ōshio Heihachirō in 1837 against what he perceived as government insensitivity to the poor during a famine. After pilfering food from the warehouses of the rich, his followers ran riot and destroyed a quarter of the city's buildings before being forcefully put down. Other protests were quieter, as in the case of northern villagers who, a chronicler said, greeted visiting officials rudely in 1788: "Some presented themselves stark naked, others bowed their heads only to raise their buttocks, and some remained inside their huts sleeping with their legs sprawled."[20] Still other actions took the form of petitions, peaceful demonstrations, or the smashing of a village headman's property. The protests, which numbered more than thirty a year during the 1780s, sought short-term solutions rather than systemic change, but they heightened the widespread perception that the social order was disintegrating.

Foreign threats also fueled the sense of crisis, as Western ships began to challenge the *bakufu* seclusion policies. In the 1790s and early 1800s, several Russian and American vessels made incursions into Japanese waters, seeking trade and safety from storms. In1808, panic set in after the British vessel *Phaeton* sailed into Nagasaki harbor, prompting the city's commissioner to commit suicide. In 1825, after another incident, the *bakufu* decreed that "whenever a foreign ship is sighted approaching any point on our coast, all persons on hand should fire on and drive it off…without hesitation. Never be caught offguard."[21] The decree was never fully enforced, and a decade later the policy was moderated. But the incursions provoked increasingly open debates about whether Tokugawa administrators were up to the challenge of dealing with the mounting foreign and domestic threats. When Britain demonstrated its military might by defeating China in the opium wars of the early 1840s, the tone of discussions became more urgent.

Analyses of the causes of these crises were as varied as the ideological camps from which their authors came. Traditionalists cited moral decline in the ruling class, arguing that "the samurai have become effeminate and resemble a body that contracts with illness after exposure to cold, wind, or heat."[22] Some young samurai blamed incompetent bureaucrats, calling officials "wooden monkeys"—like the "see no evil, hear no evil, speak no evil" carvings at Nikkō[23]—and demanding more decisive leadership. Rather ominously for the Tokugawa, *daimyō* in several of the outer domains began showing increasing (albeit discreet) signs of independence and less inclination to follow *bakufu* orders. Certain Confucian scholars urged greater practicality and innovation in matters of trade and finance, while those in the Dutch learning camp advocated a Western-style military and more interaction with the West.

Critics were united, however, in assuming that everyone belonged to a single, imperiled realm, and their varied arguments bear witness to the advent of what some call proto-nationalism. As the *bakuhan* and trade systems had integrated far-flung regions spatially, the new sense of danger united people spiritually. Confucianists speculated less about universal forces now and more about Japanese particularities. Dutch learners spoke in terms of *national* necessities. The *kokugaku* scholars talked about what made Japan special, in particular the heaven-descended imperial line that set it apart from other countries, and by extension called the legitimacy of Tokugawa rule into question. When the nationalist scholar Aizawa Seishisai began his influential 1825 collection of essays, *New Theses,* with the assertion "Our Divine Realm is where the sun emerges," a place that "rightly constitutes the head and shoulders of the world and controls all nations,"[24] he was expressing a shared sense of Japanese superiority that would have been unthinkable in the pre-Tokugawa days. Peace, new levels of national integration, and increased prosperity had come to the islands during the first two Tokugawa centuries, made possible in part by a stable regime in Edo. Now that regime had grown old and ineffective, and scholars had created a nation-oriented vocabulary to express their growing worries about the country's health—a vocabulary that would facilitate Japan's encounters with the global world after 1850.

CHAPTER 5

The Nation Transformed
(1850–1905)

I t is the warm season. On the floor of a tiny apartment sits a barefoot mother, shoulders bent, kimono soiled, an infant in her arms
and a lightly clothed youngster to her right. Behind her, her pros-
trate husband naps, shirtless, and beyond him the room opens onto
what appears to be an alley, where the family's wash hangs. The space
is cramped, the faces somber; everyone looks tired and in need of a
bath.

The scene, depicted in the 1908 oil painting *Shafu no katei* (Puller's
family) by Mitsutani Kunishirō, won people's hearts partly because of
its sensitivity to life in Tokyo's crowded slums and partly because it
portrayed a character everyone knew: the rickshaw puller. More than
100,000 pullers plied Tokyo's streets in the early 1890s, filling neighborhoods with clickety-clacks, singsongs, and curses, irritating flop-house
companions with exhausted snores during their off hours, and providing urban tales of compassion, crime, and sass. Who uses the rickshaw?
asked a reporter in 1893: "Old people. Infants. Most women. Secluded
folk. The sedentary people. Men of rank. Even the poor. There are not
many who don't ride rickshaws....One rider is prosperous; another is
old and feeble. One is obese, like a pig, another poor and thin, with legs
like mosquitoes."[1]

These larger-than-life transporters have much to tell us about the
era named Meiji (1868–1912), when Japan moved to the front ranks
of modern nations. Their labors bespoke rapid change: the migration of millions to the cities, the invention of efficient transportation,
the internationalization of the archipelago, as the pullers' customers
hailed from ever more distant parts of the globe. They also spoke to
the era's darker side, to the poverty in which most workers lived, the
crowded conditions, filth, and clamor that accompanied progress, and
the class consciousness that caused the affluent to treat their transporters like chattel. The Meiji years shine brightly in most stories, as a time
of breathtaking transformation, but any honest story must also take
account of the darker side.

There is no way to calculate how long the late Tokugawa crises might have continued, if left to the bureaucrats and critics alone, before the *bakuhan* system collapsed. It is clear, however, that change was hastened by the intrusion of a new element: foreigners determined to force the country open. On July 8, 1853, U.S. Commodore Matthew Perry sailed into Edo Bay, triggering a new wave of public debates with his demand that Japan open its ports to American vessels. When he returned for an answer the following February, this time with almost a quarter of the American navy (eight warships), the Japanese negotiated strenuously and then agreed, signing the Treaty of Kanagawa, which opened two ports for the provisioning of ships (but not for trade) and provided for an exchange of diplomats. Perry and his hosts drank toasts and exchanged gifts. One of Perry's gifts was a quarter-scale model train, which attracted crowds who, in the account of the expedition's official scribe, watched its "repeated circlings... with unabated pleasure and surprise, unable to repress a shout of delight at each blast of the steam whistle."[2] The train also induced fears—because Japan had now entered an imperialist world for which Tokugawa foreign policy had left it unprepared.

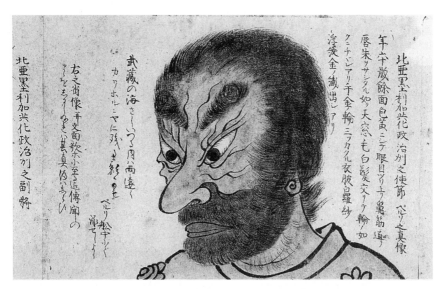

This 1853 watercolor of Matthew Perry, by an unknown Japanese artist, illustrates the way most Japanese thought of the intruding Americans: hairy, with large noses and demonic eyes. Honolulu Academy of Arts, Gift of Mrs. Walter F. Dillingham in memory of Alice Perry Grew, 1960 (2732.1).

Challenges to the shogun's government came from every direction now. First, there were the foreigners. The U.S. consul, Townsend Harris, arrived in August 1856, determined to negotiate a commercial treaty, and from then on the demands never let up. By 1858, Harris had his treaty, permitting trade and setting sharp limits on the tariffs Japan could assess; then he and other Western envoys secured promises for half a dozen additional treaty ports. By the 1860s, they had created rowdy foreign communities in Yokohama, Kobe, and Nagasaki, where merchants frequented trading houses by day, bars and brothels at night, and churches on Sunday. Most fearsome to the Japanese was the foreigners' willingness to secure their demands through force. When Satsuma domain refused to pay an indemnity after the 1862 murder of a British citizen, for example, seven English ships bombarded Kagoshima, the Satsuma capital, causing massive damage—an action described by an American reporter as "not an endeavor to establish... sound principles of civilization" but "a sordid intrigue for the benefit of British trade."[3] Behind each Western demand after the mid-1850s lay the threat of guns.

Officials also felt wave after wave of domestic opposition in these years. Peasants and common city folk bought a million copies of broadsides about the foreigners, many of them demanding expulsion of the "foreign devils." In the 1860s, they staged more than 800 uprisings, mostly to protest financial difficulties sparked by crop failures, food shortages, and inflation. In 1866, when thousands of peasants rioted over food shortages, overturning miso vats, smashing houses, and stealing cash in what is now Fukushima Prefecture, one rich farmer blamed the high interest rates charged by heartless moneylenders (he called them "leeches"), while a village headman said the rioters were motivated by class envy: "They had come to hate men of property and simply wanted to reduce them to utter poverty."[4]

Even more worrisome to the regime was the violent opposition of disaffected samurai, called *shishi* (men of valor), many of whom were studying at fencing academies in Edo and Kyoto. Upset by the foreign incursion and Tokugawa ineptitude, Yoshida Shōin, a teacher of many *shishi*, wrote, "How can any red-blooded person bear to see our great Japan, which has remained independent and unconquered for three thousand years, suddenly become enslaved by other powers?"[5] "Sonnō jōi" was the *shishi* cry: "Revere the emperor; throw out the barbarians!" Action was their motif. They came to be known on city streets for both their unwashed, unkempt personal style and their violent actions. Like terrorists of the twenty-first century, they signed blood oaths and assassinated those they held responsible for

Japan's troubles, including the regent, Ii Naosuke, who had negotiated the 1858 commercial treaties. Although their terrorism did not itself threaten the regime's existence, they created a climate in which ever more troublesome elements might flourish.

The regime's most serious threat rose from the official classes, especially the leadership in several of the largest domains. When *bakufu* officials asked advice from the *daimyō* about how to respond to Perry, they were regarded as weak for having had to ask, and as the years passed a series of *daimyō* maneuvers increasingly undermined Tokugawa authority. By the early 1860s, large *han* such as Chōshū on the western tip of Honshu and Satsuma in southern Kyushu were showing signs of independence, and after financial straits forced the Tokugawa to discontine the alternate attendance system in 1862, domain lords stopped coming regularly to Edo and their independence turned to challenge. In 1864, troops with ties to Chōshū staged an attack on Kyoto, intending to remove the emperor from the Tokugawa system and turn him into a tool for their anti-Tokugawa schemes. They failed, but their boldness inspired others, and a year later a combined peasant-samurai force toppled the relatively moderate government of Chōshū domain, placing one of Japan's five largest *han* under the control of rebels. Thereafter, Satsuma's leaders signed a secret agreement that they would not support any *bakufu* attacks on the rebel regime, and when the Tokugawa sent a punitive expedition to Chōshū in the summer of 1866, Satsuma stood aside, dooming the attacking forces to failure. Japan's leadership struggle now resembled "a ball balanced on a mountain peak," said the young rebel Kido Takayoshi, ready to "plunge downwards for thousands of feet."[6]

The final stages of the Tokugawa demise began with the Meiji Restoration of January 3, 1868, when Satsuma troops seized the palace grounds and proclaimed a new government in the name of the fifteen-year-old emperor, Mutsuhito, who now was called the emperor Meiji. They replaced the shogun with a temporary council of princes and demanded that Tokugawa lands be returned to the throne. Shogun Tokugawa Yoshinobu resisted briefly, and then decided, to the consternation of many of his followers, to submit to the new regime rather than plunge Japan into all-out civil war. "Now that foreign intercourse becomes daily more extensive," he wrote in his letter of resignation, "unless the government is directed from one central authority, the foundations of the state will fall to pieces." He said duty required him to surrender his post so that unity could be maintained.[7]

Few people expected his statesman-like statement to settle things. Many of his own followers fought on without him, in what became an eighteen-month civil war claiming 8,200 lives. The country's problems—the foreign threat, soaring debts, chaotic financial structures, rivalries among regional lords, and commoner unrest, to name a few—gave instability an air of inevitability. Yet the Meiji rebels did more than survive. They thrived, cobbling together an administration in the name of a shy teenaged emperor and turning a "restoration" into a revolution of national goals and systems. How did they do it? One answer lies in the Tokugawa legacy. Recall the high literacy rates of that era, the commercial revolution, the bustling cities, and the sophisticated intellectual sphere. Even in its last, desperate decade, the *bakufu* had engaged Westerners rather than merely resisting them, Chinese-style. Big as the problems were, the Meiji innovators inherited a structure with strong foundations.

Another explanation lies in the men who took charge in 1868, a coterie that included a few court nobles and a larger group of young samurai from southern and western domains, especially Chōshū and Satsuma. The oldest, Prince Iwakura Tomomi and the Satsuma samurai Saigō Takamori, were only in their early forties, and none had top-level administrative experience. What they shared, however, was vision, talent, and realism, along with a commitment to nation-building. Advocating slogans such as "*Kuni no tame*" (for the good of the country) and "*Fukoku kyōhei*" (rich country/strong army), they threw themselves into consolidating the new regime. Their pragmatism was illustrated by their approach to the West. Most of this leadership group had entered public life as ideologues, passionate about ridding Japan of the barbarians. Now, in power, they concluded realistically that expulsion was impossible; Japan must compete with the West on its own terms. So when they issued a "charter oath" on April 6, outlining the Meiji government's principles, they promised: "knowledge shall be sought throughout the world," "matters of state shall be decided by public discussion," and "classes high and low shall unite."[8] They issued the proclamation in a formal Shintō ceremony—evidence that they understood the political wisdom of clothing modern policies in comfortable traditional symbols.

Two contrasting, equally crucial tasks occupied officials during the first Meiji decade: destroying old structures and building new ones. Facing a world that required not just stability but diplomatic, business, and military prowess, the Meiji leaders saw much in the Tokugawa order that would not work. The geographic separation of the imperial palace

(Kyoto) and administrative center (Edo), for example, contained the seeds of intrigue; so they brought the emperor to Edo and renamed the city Tokyo. The *han* structure burdened—and threatened—the country with hundreds of regional governments, each with its own army and tax system. To deal with that, the officials first persuaded, then coerced, the regional lords to submit their domains to the emperor and give up the title of *daimyō*. The process provoked opposition, but by balancing military threats with financial inducements, the Meiji rulers succeeded in turning 261 domains into 302 prefectures, which were later reshaped into 72 prefectures and three urban districts. Another impediment to modernity was the Tokugawa status system, under which the two million samurai lived on government stipends. Not only did the stipends consume 30 percent of the national budget, they reinforced the anachronistic class divisions. The Meiji government confronted this problem in several ways. In 1869, it replaced the status system with three categories: nobles, samurai, and commoners (a designation that included everyone from farmers to former outcasts), and in 1870 it allowed commoners to take surnames, a right that previously had belonged to samurai alone. Then the officials abolished the warrior class itself, decreeing in 1876 that ex-samurai must stop wearing swords and that after being given a final, interest-bearing bond, they no longer would receive government funds. While most grudgingly accepted the reforms, samurai in several provinces rose in rebellion. In 1877, the now disillusioned Saigō was persuaded by Kyushu followers to lead the massive Satsuma Rebellion, which lasted eight months and cost 30,000 lives. When army chief Yamagata Aritomo looked at the fallen Saigō that October and said, "Now I am at peace,"[9] he was thinking about Japan as much as about himself; for with this hero's death had come the end of armed resistance to the new regime.

Even as the dismantling process continued, the Meiji leaders were furiously creating new institutions to centralize control and modernize Japan. They experimented with several ruling structures, eventually creating a Council of State under which cabinet-style ministries operated. They constructed railroads and telegraph lines, created experimental factories, adopted the Western calendar, built an effective postal system, devised administrative structures to bring the far-flung provinces under closer control, and encouraged the growth of a press—all the while struggling to stabilize the country's desperate financial situation.

The engine for these changes was wholly Japanese. Many of the models, by contrast, came from Europe and the United States. Recognizing that much of the world's wealth and power resided on the other side of the globe, officials began examining Western ideas and institutions with an enthusiasm that called to mind Suiko and Shōtoku Taishi sending missions to seventh-century China. During the 1870s, they invited thousands of well-paid foreigners to teach and give advice: surveyors and engineers, English and geology teachers, advisors on educational policy, constitutional theorists, newspaper editors. The Japanese went West, too, sending promising young men—and occasionally, women—to study in American and European secondary schools and colleges, and sponsoring short-term professional missions to observe banks, schools, and weapons factories. Most impressive was the 1871–1873 Iwakura Mission, in which fifty leaders, including five top officials, spent eighteen months traveling throughout the West to observe foreign affairs, negotiate treaties, and report to the rest of the world on Japan's progress. Many things befuddled the travelers, including Christians worshiping crucifixes "profuse with ruby-red blood" and women "wearing men's clothes." Following one social event, mission secretary Kume Kunitake remarked, "To our eyes the sight of the young men dancing in the embrace of women after the music began was extremely indecent." If this was the way of the future, he said, "the Way of Loyalty and Filial Piety will be in peril."[10] But the journey's most remarkable aspect lay in the mere fact that it happened, that officials considered Western models important enough to leave Japan for such a long time, even as their regime was still finding its feet.

All of this study inspired a wave of westernization in the 1870s. Referred to as *bunmei kaika* (civilization and enlightenment), the onslaught inundated Japan with barber shops, beef eating, literary translations (the Bible, Shakespeare, Jules Verne), brick buildings, beer guzzling, dairy farms (even in the city), ideas such as individualism and natural rights, wristwatches, and girls' schools—as well as a government-sponsored hall where Kume's worries must have seemed prescient as Japanese and foreigners congregated for Western ballroom dancing and masked balls. An English resident of Tokyo quipped, "Old things pass away between a night and a morning. The Japanese boast that they have done in thirty or forty years what it took Europe half as many centuries to accomplish."[11] Few disputed him.

Accompanying *bunmei kaika* was a host of new institutions designed to help Japan compete with the West. First came an 1872 law—the world's first—making four years of school compulsory for all girls and boys. Decades would be required for full implementation, partly because schools were costly and partly because many farmers opposed the intrusion of schools into their family work calendars, with villagers in some

Opened in 1890, the twelve-story, 225-foot-high Ryōunkaku (Cloud Scraper), depicted in this woodblock print by Ichijū Kunimasa, was Tokyo's tallest building and foremost tourist attraction. Equipped with Japan's first elevator, it was filled with shops selling goods from around the world, and topped by two observatory floors, complete with telescopes. Edo Tokyo Hakubutsukan; no. 88132878.

areas even burning the new school buildings down. But the measure illustrated the modernizers' conviction that education was essential to successful nation-building. Two equally controversial, equally fundamental, changes came in 1873: a 3 percent land tax (later reduced to 2.5 percent) to standardize the revenue system, and a military draft, requiring males to provide three years of service followed by four years in the reserves, beginning at age twenty. The draft was widely regarded as a "blood tax" on commoners, because the rich could buy their way out.

If these reforms were intended to lay the groundwork for a modern state, another innovation was designed to assure loyalty by appealing to largely fabricated traditions. The one-time rebel Kido, now a leader in the new government, wrote in his diary on March 11, 1868, that in order "to establish a foundation for the Empire enduring for all ages," he had "quietly been making efforts to clarify the principle that the focus of the highest loyalty should be fixed on the Emperor."[12] Agreeing with him, the Meiji rulers created a host of ceremonies and institutions—many of them new, though they appeared old—to turn the emperor simultaneously into a sovereign, a high priest, and a loving father. They made Shintō into a state religion, pressuring some Buddhist temples to become Shintō shrines and requiring priests to teach respect for the nation and its *kami*. They also created holidays celebrating the nation, sent the emperor on visits among the people, commissioned a national song, and created a new shrine, Yasukuni, to the war dead. The impact of these programs, many of which were modeled on the Western governments' use of Christianity, would continue long after the end of the Meiji era.

The early Meiji officials struggled hardest, perhaps, to create a constitutional system. Early in 1874, after Saigō had left the government over its handling of foreign affairs and its insensitivity to samurai concerns, several of his supporters sent a memorial to the throne demanding a legislature on the grounds that "the people whose duty it is to pay taxes to the government have the right of sharing in their government's affairs."[13] The petition touched off a firestorm of discussion, giving rise to the *jiyū minken* (freedom and people's rights) crusade, Japan's first popular political movement. For nearly a decade, former samurai and wealthy agriculturalists agitated for an assembly and a constitution, while officials debated what kind of constitutional system Japan should have. As journalist Fukuchi Gen'ichirō wrote, "The discussion about a popular assembly has become like *Forty-Seven Masterless Warriors* at the theater; whatever the date or the weather, there is always a full house."[14]

A turning point in the process came in mid-1881, when a corruption scandal over the sale of government-developed lands in Hokkaido triggered another popular outburst, with *jiyū minken* activists declaring that without a constitution or a legislature, government could not be held to account. Stunned by the furor, officials stopped the sale and promised to establish an assembly in 1890. The activists then began forming political parties in anticipation of coming elections, while officials began working on a constitution under the supervision of Itō Hirobumi (another rebel turned official) and with the assistance of several German advisors. In addition to writing constitutional drafts, officials also created new institutions, such as a cabinet and a peerage system, to ensure a smooth path toward constitutional government. Their most controversial—and troubling—creation was the draconian Peace Regulations of December 1887, which banished some 570 activists from Tokyo on the pretext that they were a threat to national order.

The emperor Meiji promulgated the constitution, Asia's first, on February 11, 1889, a day marked by festivals at home and praise abroad. The document was moderately conservative, creating a sovereign emperor who appointed the cabinet members and held final legislative power over everything but the budget. At the same time, it created a popularly elected legislature, the Diet, along with an independent judiciary, and it gave the Diet the crucial right to veto budgets. People would argue for decades about how democratic the document was, but all regarded it as a monumental step toward modernity. "Where there is a nation there is necessarily a constitution," a provincial editorialist wrote.[15] Japan had become a nation indeed, and for the first time, the people would have a formal voice in national decision-making—a loud and insistent one, as the 1890s would show.

One reason so many people had come to see constitutional government as essential was that modernity had now reached nearly every part of society, nurtured as much by private forces as by government officials. Businessmen built factories and installed electric lights in the mid-Meiji years so they could keep laborers working all night in twelve-hour shifts. Distant governors created English-language schools and lobbied for funds to build dams. Activist women joined the people's rights movement and schemed to export "civilization" to Korea. Capitalistic journalists devised sales gimmicks to secure readers. Farmers grumbled about the solar calendar but used the latest tools and fertilizers to increase their annual harvests. Children in rural provinces repeated rumors that meat-eating gave foreigners a "peculiar animal odour"; then, on being given their own first bite of meat, "confided to each other that we liked the taste."[16]

For many groups, the era's changes brought more hardships than benefits, at least in the short run. While some women, for example, enjoyed new political opportunities, tens of thousands were sent off to work in textile factories, where the salaries were paltry, working conditions were cruel, and crowded dorms were filthy. Suicides and desertions were common, and most of the female workers, many in their early teens, empathized with one who recalled, "I don't know how many times I thought I would rather jump into Lake Suwa and drown."[17] Even middle-class women often found their lives more restricted now, as officials bent on creating a stable system began demanding that women marry and stay at home as "good wives and wise mothers." After 1890, female participation in politics was banned altogether.

Most farmers, too, saw times grow worse with the adoption of the land tax, which made them responsible for more than 80 percent of the

Villagers walk home after a day of farming, about 1900. The farmer in front carries the plow pulled in the fields by the horse. City life may have turned modern, but rural life remained much as it had been for generations. Photograph courtesy Peabody Essex Museum, Salem, Massachusetts, A5132.

government's revenue. After finance minister Matsukata Masayoshi responded to debts and inflation by raising taxes and decreasing the currency in circulation in the early 1880s, many farmers fell into destitution. "Poor farmers withered up like the vegetation around them," a village teacher commented a few years later. "While the frogs and insects hibernated peacefully, farmers had to consume their meager stores of grain just to keep themselves alive from day to day. Inevitably a time would come when they had nothing left to eat."[18] Record numbers began protesting. *Burakumin*, as the former outcasts now were called, also suffered bitterly, sometimes from ongoing discrimination and almost always from hard living conditions. And

An old fisherman, photographed in about 1890, wears the rough cotton jacket—and wizened face—typical of his profession. Photograph courtesy Peabody Essex Museum, Salem, Massachusetts.

then there were the coal miners, sent into the earth to work naked, or in loincloths, in temperatures up to 120 degrees, to produce fuel for the modernizing factories—and for export. Newspapers reported frequently on mine explosions and cave-ins that took countless lives. The miners' miseries were compounded by coldhearted officials, such as the one who recommended convicts for mine work in the 1880s because "if they keep dying from this work, it will just decrease their numbers."[19]

By contrast, these years smiled on the entrepreneurial classes, who lived largely free of taxes. The first Meiji decades saw the steady growth of an increasingly diverse economy. A silkworm blight in Europe allowed the Japanese to begin exporting first cocoons and then silk threads in great quantities after the late 1860s. Silk made up more than a third of Japan's early Meiji exports. Industrial production expanded more slowly, but by the era's third decade, manufacturing was growing 5 percent a year, while coal production increased ten times between 1874 and 1888, to more than two million tons. Railway lines were laid with impressive speed, too: in 1872, Japan had eighteen miles of tracks; by century's end, it boasted nearly 4,000, three-quarters of it in private hands.[20] The entrepreneur Shibusawa Eiichi, who founded more than fifty companies, used the rhetoric of the Meiji merchant class when he proclaimed that "the secret to success in business is the determination to work for the sake of society and of mankind as well as for the future of the nation, even if it means sacrificing oneself."[21] He used the methods of that class when he subjected girls at his Osaka Spinning Mill to inhuman hours and low wages. Profit had become Japan's bottom line.

By the late 1880s, the foundations of modern Japan had largely been laid. During the next two decades, the country saw an explosion of two relatively new forces: nationalism and mass urban culture. Several factors lay behind the former, including an understandable pride in the early Meiji achievements and the ever-greater efforts of officials to nurture loyalty. "There are two indispensable elements in the field of foreign policy," education minister-to-be Inoue Kowashi wrote; "the armed forces first and education second. If the Japanese people are not imbued with patriotic spirit, the nation cannot be strong."[22] To that end, he and others drafted the best known document of that generation, the 1890 Imperial Rescript on Education, which made loyalty to the emperor and respect for parents the basis of education. Recited at important school functions, much like the Pledge of Allegiance in the United States, it reinforced the view that love of the emperor was an ancient tradition, even though most Japanese had known next to nothing about their emperors before Meiji.

Another source of nationalism was resentment of the West, particularly among younger Japanese tired of hearing about foreign superiority. "A Westerner abroad takes pride in his country," wrote one young scholar in 1890; "not so with our countryman. When a [Japanese] comes in contact with foreigners, he is like a mouse emerging hesitantly on a bright morning."[23] For others, the resentment sprang from humiliating experiences under the unequal treaties that had been imposed on Japan in the 1850s: from anger over Japan's inability to set its own tariffs, and from indignation about extraterritoriality, which deprived Japan of legal jurisdiction over foreigners living in Japan. Antiforeign sentiment peaked when the British captain of the ship *Normanton* let all twenty-three of its Japanese passengers drown in an 1886 shipwreck while saving himself and his crew, and then was absolved by Britain's consular court in Kobe.[24]

Struggles over relations with neighbors also raised national consciousness—and with it, patriotism—in the early Meiji years. Officials began clarifying Japan's borders by establishing a colonial office in the newly named northern island of Hokkaido in 1869; they poured millions of yen into development of the area and sent two million "mainlanders" there, even as they drove the native Ainu, widely thought to have had ancient links to the Emishi, from their homes. Four years later, in 1873, the regime provoked a major split in the government when it blocked a scheme by Saigō to invade Korea. A year after that, officials won wide domestic acclaim for sending troops to southern Taiwan, ostensibly to punish mountaineers who had massacred fifty-four shipwrecked Ryūkyūans, but really to back up Japan's claim of suzerainty over the Ryūkyūs, which long had been an independent kingdom with close ties to both China and Japan. When Japan forcibly turned the Ryūkyū chain into Okinawa Prefecture in 1879, over vigorous Chinese objections, the domestic press again was overwhelmingly supportive. All of these border-defining moves made it clear that the early Meiji officials were interested as much in international matters as in domestic programs. The moves also fueled national pride.

Nationalist sentiments soared in the mid-1890s when Japan and China fought over Korea. Following Perry's pattern, Japan had forced Korea in 1876 to sign a commercial treaty, and thereafter China and Japan clashed repeatedly on the peninsula, with the Chinese emphasizing their historic ties to Korea and Japan proclaiming its desire to "civilize" the country. The two came close to war in the mid-1880s before negotiations quieted things. Then in the spring of 1894, when China responded positively (and in line with treaty stipulations), to Korea's request for military aid in quelling a domestic uprising, Japan's press turned jingoistic, demanding that China be challenged. When the Japanese cabinet deliberated about what to do, the newspaper *Ōsaka Asahi* worried that Japan was missing a providential opportunity to assert itself in Asia: "If we lose this chance, all ages will regret it....We should take the lead in making Korea's independence clear; instead we look on in a daze."[25]

Hostilities began in July; the Sino-Japanese War was declared on August 1; and by late autumn Japan had won such smashing victories that China was suing for peace. When a peace treaty was signed the following April 17, Japan received Taiwan and southern Manchuria's Liaodong Peninsula, as well as a large indemnity and extensive commercial rights in China. More important than the victory, however, were two wartime developments that would reverberate in succeeding decades. The first occurred in Port Arthur, where Japanese troops massacred hundreds of civilians after defeating the Chinese. Tokyo launched an investigation and apologized, but foreign reporters expressed shock and outrage. Even more significant was the explosion of patriotic fervor the war ignited at home. "The excitement generated among the Japanese people was beyond imagination," the commentator Ubukata Toshirō recalled; "every adult, every child, every elderly person, every woman talked day and night of nothing but the war."[26] By war's end, Japan had become a different place: proud of defeating Asia's giant, confident in its military might, thirsty for more territory. The thirst grew even stronger days after the conclusion of peace, when Japan was coerced by Russia, Germany, and France, which had interests of their own, to give Liaodong back to China. Called the Triple Intervention, the episode sparked another public explosion, with editorialists across the political spectrum damning the cabinet for giving in to the European trio and declaring that Japan must strengthen itself so that it could stand up to Westerners in the future. "Having been crushed now," one said, "we will have our chance to succeed another day."[27]

The postwar years saw a rush of support for this vision of strength, even as Japan's cities became both modern and massive. While the rural regions lost population, Japan's metropolises grew by a combined 10 million in the last two decades of the 1800s, with Tokyo reaching more than 2.5 million by 1910 and Osaka nearly 2 million. In part, that reflected a rise in industry—and city jobs—as the Sino-Japanese War indemnity poured more than 360 million yen into the economy. Exports tripled in the 1890s; imports quadrupled; factories quintupled. As a result, by early in the twentieth century the number of Japan's workers had doubled to more than a million—three-fifths of them women. Many economists call this the takeoff stage of Japan's first industrial revolution.

As the cities grew, they changed in nature. People became better educated, with male literacy passing the 90 percent mark at the turn of the century and female literacy reaching 82 percent. They also became newspaper readers, subscribing to papers that were cheap, sensational, and easy to read. And they became increasingly active in looking out for themselves, ready to struggle publicly for better wages and working conditions. In the 1890s, scores of strikes and protests broke out in Japan's major cities, while workers at the Furukawa copper mine in Ashio north of Tokyo staged Japan's first antipollution protests. The miners also protested pollution and working conditions in 1907, laying waste to scores of buildings before government troops stopped the violence. One miner was overheard telling his fellows: "There must be no looting, because that would shame us. But let's make sure we smash everything thoroughly."[28]

One cause of the urban activism lay in the concentration of workers in city slums, where families of four typically shared a three-mat (fifty-four- square-foot) room without indoor cooking facilities or toilets, while their poorer friends stayed in flophouses where the summer air reeked of sweat and the winter "wind came through the cracks, penetrating until you couldn't bear it." The middle classes saw these people as "an almost subhuman species only slightly related to other human beings,"[29] in the words of one journalist. In truth, they represented Japan's future, sending their children to city schools and demanding, increasingly, to be treated not just as humans but as citizens. All the while, the more affluent classes were changing the face of Japan's cities with their electric lights, their erudite opinion journals, and their attraction to fashionable department stores. Between 1889 and 1900, Japan's cities produced the country's first beer halls, first multistory observation towers, and first movies, as well as Japan's own Ebisu beer, not to mention a toilet stool that played music. Magazines like *Taiyō* (The sun) offered social commentary interspersed with ads for everything from cigarettes to fire insurance. The circulations of some individual newspapers rose to 250,000 by the end of Meiji. And the annual blossom-viewing festivals and fireworks displays brought people together from every part of the country.

For the authorities, this class-mingling and activism conjured up visions of a breakdown in values, even revolution, so they worked assiduously to constrain potential opposition and promote national strength. When the leftist Social Democratic Party was formed in 1901, the government shut it down, and when *Heimin Shimbun*, a Marxist newspaper, appeared two years later, the bureaucrats

Rickshaw pullers were among the most common sights in Japanese cities of the late 1800s. They came from the poorest classes, carried people from every walk of life, and became legendary for their strong, irrepressible personalities. By the 1920s, they had been replaced by streetcars and automobiles. This photo was taken early in the 1880s. Photograph courtesy of Peabody Essex Museum, Salem, Massachusetts, A9053.

watched for a year and then banished it, too. In the effort to project strength, officials devoted 40 percent of the country's annual budgets to building the army and navy between 1896 and 1903, and in 1900 the government adopted a regulation that only generals or admirals on active duty could serve in the cabinet, a move that gave the military a virtual veto over the formation of the cabinet. When Japan provided roughly half of the international force that put down China's Boxer Rebellion in 1900, and then shared handsomely in the indemnity, the pride that had marked the Sino-Japanese War was reignited. That pride showed itself again two years later when Japan signed the Anglo-Japanese Alliance, recognizing Great Britain's predominance in China in return for the British recognition of Japan's key role in Korea. Intended as a restraint on Russian expansion in the East, it was the first equal alliance between Asian and European powers.

Ironically, this expansiveness stimulated insecurity as often as pride, with each advance inviting a worrisome challenge. In the new colony of Taiwan, for example, 4,600 Japanese soldiers were killed putting down local resistance, and the cost of running the colony sapped Tokyo's finances in the late 1890s. In Seoul, where the Japanese had expected to push reforms through easily after driving China out, Korean officials resisted, prompting the Japanese minister to assassinate Korea's recalcitrant Queen Min, and the Koreans, in turn, to seek protection from Russia. In China, the Japanese felt threatened—and angered—in the late 1890s when Russia used treaties to grasp control of Liaodong, the very peninsula it had pressured Japan to give back. When Russia moved troops into the peninsula after the Boxer Rebellion, journalists demanded that steps be taken to resist Russian expansion and assure Korea's "independence." If the government would not stand up to Russia, the prominent editor Tokutomi Sohō predicted late in 1903, "the righteous indignation of our people could not be held back."[30]

The rising tension led to Japanese-Russian negotiations, and when talks failed, the Russo-Japanese War broke out on February 8, 1904, with Japan's surprise attack on Russian ships at Liaodong's Port Arthur. This was a very different conflict from the Sino-Japanese War. It was much longer and much larger; it pitted Japan against a Western power; and the results were less clear-cut. Over seventeen months, the conflict threw up staggering statistics for Japan: more than a million troops mobilized, more than 1.5 billion yen expended (half of it borrowed from foreigners), and 100,000 troops killed. The battles were massive. Japan's victorious, eight-month siege of Port Arthur resulted in more than 90,000 casualties. The battle for Mukden (Shenyang), which followed in March 1905, pitted 250,000 Japanese against 320,000 Russians. Though Japan won again, it suffered 70,000 casualties and used up nearly all of its resources. Only a stunning naval victory over Russia's fleet in the Tsushima Straits in late May gave Japan the victory, and even then the peace treaty, mediated by U.S. president Theodore Roosevelt and signed in September at Portsmouth, New Hampshire, failed to yield either an indemnity or as much territory as Japanese expansionists craved.

The treaty did recognize Japan's "paramount interest" in Korea and transferred Russia's Manchurian holdings to Japan, along with the southern half of Sakhalin island; it also pushed Japan into the ranks of world leadership. But that was not enough for a public that had become clamorously patriotic. When the treaty produced no indemnity, editorialists lambasted the negotiators, and citizens erupted in a rage more violent than after the Triple Intervention. A huge Tokyo demonstration on September 5 turned into three days of rioting. The next month, a different yet equally patriotic sentiment drew even more Tokyoites to Ueno Park, this time to welcome the navy home from war. Clearly, two contrasting commitments had taken hold of Japan's people by 1905: a nearly universal belief in Japan's right to assert itself abroad and a widespread commitment to the citizen's right to express personal convictions in the public arena.

The contrast between the early years of the twentieth century and the beginning of the Meiji era challenges one's imaginative powers. In 1868, the capital's population had numbered about 500,000; now it exceeded two million. Then, the government had been run by rebels; now, offices were allocated under a constitutional system. Provincial samurai had used swords against the Tokugawa; today, soldiers had defeated a Western power with modern weapons. Once cowering, Japan had become audacious. The material change was monumental too: the rich now enjoyed modern water systems, ate under electric lights, and talked on telephones. The middle classes went to movies, read newspapers, and listened to phonographs. The poor lived in urban slums or hardscrabble villages yet sent their children to public schools to study English and math with their affluent peers. History's harsh reality tells us that modernity had other narratives yet to spin, that it was about to thrust Japan into a maelstrom. Now, however, in the afterglow of victory over Russia, the Meiji story spoke primarily of transformation. Japan had become modern—and mighty.

CHAPTER 6

Engaging the World, for Good and for Ill (1905–1945)

Our Reporter Hashimoto Shigeru—Slashed by Police Officers," proclaimed the *Tokyo Nichi Nichi* newspaper on Wednesday, February 11, 1914.[1] Hashimoto, whose bandaged visage accompanied the story, had been covering a protest rally at Tokyo's Hibiya Park the previous day when policemen had stabbed him. A few days later, security guards beat up another journalist, who was seeking information at the home minister's residence. In both cases, the authorities were skittish about press stories regarding bribes taken by naval officials from the German industrial and engineering conglomerate Siemens.

Public outrage over the bribes and bullying toppled the cabinet; the whole episode showed how complicated Japan's public life had become in the early twentieth century. First, there were the people on the streets—40,000 of them at that rally. By the 1910s, Japan's masses had become citizens, demanding a hearing on issues such as taxes, prices, and corruption. The people's era had arrived. But it was not that simple; the police reactions suggested another feature of these years: the authorities' determination to maintain control at any cost. The scandal suggested a third theme: Japan's integration into the international sphere. The bribery deal, between Germans and Japanese, was uncovered when a Tokyo worker sold documents to a British journalist. All of these forces—engaged commoners, authoritarianism, contorted international relations—would interact in shifting patterns across the first half of Japan's twentieth century to make the Meiji years seem tranquil by comparison.

When Meiji died in July 1912, people mourned a man whose dignified persona had captured an era, a half-century that propelled Japan along a relatively straight path to world prominence. His son, the emperor Taishō, who reigned from 1912 to 1926, would preside over a different period, a mere decade and a half that exploded with competing, conflicting energies.

The explosion was most apparent in urban Japan. Metropolises continued their late Meiji growth, while new technologies and institutions revolutionized the cities' appearance and rhythms. By the end of the 1920s, a quarter of Japan's urban homes had radios; Tokyo's central train station was as modern as any in Europe, its subway the first in Asia. Equally significant, more than a fifth of Tokyoites now called themselves middle class, affluent enough to spark a blaze of consumerism. Multistory department stores went up in the 1910s, with elevators, escalators, and glass showcases containing everything from fountain pens to lipstick. Shoppers purchased the latest dresses, the most fashionable cigarettes, and the newest gadgets. Young people created a café culture, which embraced every pleasure imaginable: drinking, moviegoing, jazz, fashion consciousness, sex. Reporters dubbed it the world of *ero guro nansensu*—the erotic, the grotesque, and the nonsensical. At its center were the *mobo* (modern boy) and, even more important, the *moga* (modern girl), who dressed modishly and demanded sexual freedom—a Western-style woman like

By the beginning of the Taishō era in 1912, electric lines crowded city skyscapes and streetcars had became the fastest form of urban transportation. At left is the Shinbashi Hakuhinkan, built in 1899, which housed a collection of different shops, much like the shopping centers of a later era; it is regarded as a forerunner of Japan's first department stores. Photograph courtesy Peabody Essex Museum, Salem, Massachusetts.

Aguri in Tanizaki Jun'ichirō's 1922 short story of that name, who "imagines herself... fixing jewels on her ears, hanging a necklace around her throat, slipping into a near-transparent blouse of rustling silk or cambric, swaying elegantly on tiptoes in fragile high-heeled shoes."[2]

A remarkable feature of Taishō urban culture was its embrace of people from all classes and regions. As one journalist said of the period's proliferating beer halls, everyone "drinks the same beer as everyone else. Jinrikisha men [rickshaw pullers] meet gentlemen, workers meet merchant princes, and frock coats touch army uniforms.... Smiles blossom as beer and foam disappear into people's mouths."[3] The mass media particularly facilitated this class mingling. By the mid-1920s, several Osaka and Tokyo papers had daily circulations of nearly a million, with readers from all income groups. Magazines like *King* and *Success* attracted up to 1.5 million readers each, with tabloid-style gossip and articles on achieving success. Women's journals proliferated, running instructions on household management alongside fashion advice and rumors about stars' sexual escapades. A "mountain hamlet" reader wrote in to say that *Housewife's Companion* was "the only friend I have to teach me about all the new things going on in the world."[4]

This exploding urban culture was described and analyzed endlessly by intellectuals. The most astute chroniclers may have been the writers of "I novels," who produced individualistic, confessional writing, much of it about what the novelist Kambayashi Akatsuki called the "monster of loneliness" that "dwells deep within the human heart, and... cannot be appeased."[5] The most insistent analysts, though, were the social commentators, whose critiques ranged from hand-wringing over hedonism to condemnation of the ongoing, pervasive discrimination against groups like Hokkaido's Ainu, the still-sequestered *burakumin* communities, and Korean immigrants, who numbered nearly 300,000 by the end of the 1920s. Writers also debated the changing roles of women. In 1911, a new women's journal named *Seitō* (Blue stockings) began its first issue with the declaration "In the beginning, woman was the sun.... Today, woman is the moon, dependent on others for her birth, radiant only in others' light."[6] Over the next two decades, writers for *Seitō* and other journals debated gender issues vigorously, with traditionalists calling for a return to the "good wife/wise mother" ideal and progressives demanding equality and sexual freedom. Journalists also discussed the growing numbers of women who were themselves making news: the international track star Hitomi Kinue; the women's suffrage activist Ichikawa Fusae; and the free-living actress Matsui Sumako, who played Nora in the Japanese version of Henrik Ibsen's play *A Doll's House*.

The Taishō social vibrancy was made possible in part by a strong, if uneven, economy. The net domestic product grew by 60 percent in the decade after 1910, and industrial output quintupled, to nearly 7 billion yen. By the late 1920s, Japan had become heavily industrialized, with manufacturing surpassing agricultural output. Unfortunately, the process was spasmodic, as growth spurts were followed by downturns; one significant decline came after World War I, another after the Great Kantō Earthquake of 1923, which destroyed three-fifths of the homes in Yokohama and Tokyo and claimed nearly 140,000 lives, even as it tore apart the region's transportation, industrial, and firefighting systems. A grim joke made the rounds that fall—that "we have earthquakes for breakfast, dinner, supper, and earthquakes to sleep upon."[7] Many found it difficult even to chuckle though, for the disaster left 1.9 million people homeless and sent the economy into a temporary tailspin. What was more, economic benefits were spread unequally across the Taishō years, with wages declining for workers in smaller industries, inflation hurting the majority, and government imports of cheap rice hitting farmers hard, particularly after World War I.

These economic inequalities spurred activism and protests among consumers and workers. In the summer of 1918, for example, when wartime inflation pushed up rice prices, a million people staged protests across the islands, many of them violent. More than 300,000 renters had joined tenant unions by the mid-1920s to fight high rents and bad housing. Labor organizations flourished, as workers fought against low wages and capricious management. "I was psychologically on the verge of exploding," munitions worker Uchida Tōshida said. "The arsenal was rigidly stratified and those on the bottom stayed on the bottom. There were many wrong and unfair practices."[8] Like thousands of others, he joined Japan's first major union, the Yūaikai (Friendly Society). While unions initially emphasized moderate goals such as worker solidarity, they became more aggressive after a federation of labor organizations was created in 1919. The period's largest strike, by 27,000 Kobe shipyard workers in the summer of 1921, lasted for six weeks and sparked violent clashes between workers and police.

This activism in turn prompted wide-ranging debates about how the political system should be adapted to accommodate a changing citizenry. The most influential theorists, Yoshino Sakuzō and Minobe Tatsukichi, advocated, respectively, *minponshugi* (people-based democracy) and an "organ theory" of governance that treated the emperor as just one of several state organs—a key one, but not the entire body and soul of the state, as traditionalists had long insisted. Less mainstream was an emerging cadre of socialists, whose views ranged from the anarchism of Kōtoku Shūsui and Kanno Suga, who were executed following secret trials in 1911 for a plot against the emperor, to the Christian-Marxist blend of the economist Kawakami Hajime. In between were communist workers like Tanno Setsu, who wrote in 1928: "Woman workers! Farm women! We must realize that our living conditions will not improve merely by fighting the capitalists and the landlords.... We ... must ... fight the government as well."[9] While officials harassed the socialists, the Taishō milieu provided space for all but the most radical to speak out.

At the practical level, commoners entered the political sphere in greater numbers than ever. At first, their engagement took place mostly on the streets, where they demonstrated, often quite effectively, for a wide range of causes. In 1906, citizens protested streetcar fare increases; in 1908, they fought higher taxes; in 1913 and 1914, high-handed, corrupt government; and in 1918, rice prices. They also demonstrated repeatedly for a broader role in decision-making, insisting on the removal of all tax requirements from an electoral law that kept three-quarters of adult males from voting. A few even demanded the vote for women. Until mid-Taishō, prime ministers were selected by a group of patriarchs called the *genrō* (elder statesmen). But when the cabinet was toppled by the rice riots in 1918, the *genrō* decided that the only way to restore calm was to make the head of the majority political party, Hara Kei, prime minister. And once they had made that decision, there was no going back. For all but two of the next fourteen years, the head of the leading party would be prime minister. When the Diet passed a universal male suffrage bill in 1925, quadrupling the electorate to twelve million, most observers concluded that democracy had moved off the streets and into the voting booth.

Social energy and rising democracy were not, however, the period's sole features. Challenging every defender of café culture or worker rights was a traditionalist worried about order and power, someone who argued, like one official in 1913, that "political party fever is poisoning the provinces."[10] And the authorities did more than moan; they attempted to counter radical thoughts by nurturing patriotism and conservative values. In 1911, for example, the government created a Committee on Literature to give awards to those who wrote "wholesome" works. The plan foundered when several respected writers damned it as an attempt to control art, but the effort made clear the traditionalists' determination to safeguard the old ways. During the Taishō years, officials channeled funds to conservative elements in *burakumin* organizations, created a Harmonization Society to foster management-worker cooperation, and threw their prestige behind the expanding Patriotic Women's Society. They added martial training to the school curriculum in 1925, with a military officer assigned to each middle school. And they created an Imperial Military Reservist Association to foster patriotic values in local communities.

Officials also used more repressive means to assure conformity. Censorship of "dangerous" speeches and publications became pervasive in the 1920s, and efforts to suppress socialism increased, especially after mid-decade. From 1918 to 1930, some 350 newspapers a year were banned for articles that threatened public order, and following the 1923 earthquake, police arrested socialists and spread xenophobic rumors that led to the massacre of several thousand Korean residents by vigilantes. Military police also murdered several jailed socialists in the earthquake's aftermath. This bare-knuckled approach intensified after the passage in April 1925 of a "peace preservation law" that provided for up to ten years' imprisonment for persons who sought to abolish the private property system or change Japan's *kokutai* (national polity). A special law enforcement division, the Special Higher Police, known popularly as the "thought police," was charged with administering the law, and while enforcement was uneven in the 1920s, radical thought became increasingly unacceptable. On the night of March 15, 1928, police raided more than a hundred locations and took 1,600 suspected communists into custody.

Nothing illustrated the Taishō clash between progressive and conservative forces more vividly than Japan's actions in the arena of foreign affairs, where progressive internationalists largely held sway through the 1920s, agreeing with the diplomat Makino Nobuaki that Japan should "honor pacifism and reject aggression," in keeping with "trends of the world."[11] In that spirit, Japan joined the League of Nations and signed history's first international arms limitation agreement, the Washington Naval Treaty of 1922, despite wide concern that the treaty's five-five-three formula allowed Japan to maintain only 60 percent of the warship tonnage permitted the Americans and the British. Japan also eschewed military interference in China's domestic affairs during the 1920s and pursued peaceful relations with the Soviets.

This cooperative approach did not, however, signify a rejection of empire-building. National policy remained committed to the late Meiji goals of developing colonies and maintaining equality with the world's powers. Even as Japanese officials cooperated with the Western giants, they had no more compunction against expansive moves than the Europeans and Americans did—a fact illustrated by their actions during

World War I. In 1915, for example, they took advantage of Europe's preoccupation with the war to issue to China a set of Twenty-one Demands intended to extend Japan's leases in Manchuria and assure themselves control of important segments of Chinese affairs. China's response, which was to accept all but the most egregious demands, demonstrated Japan's potency in the region. While the Japanese stayed out of the European fighting, they carried out several military operations in

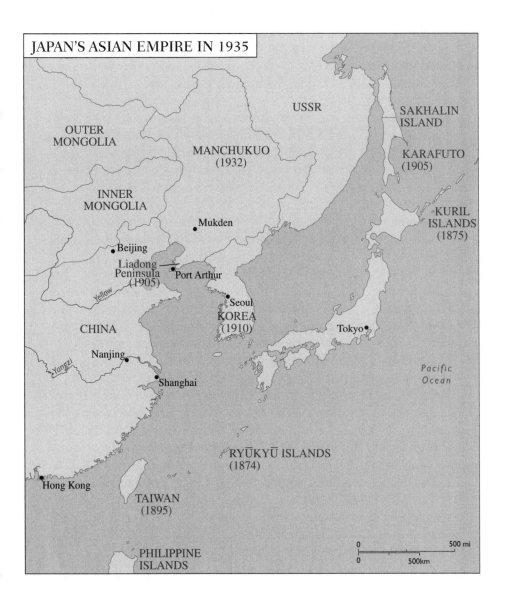

JAPAN'S ASIAN EMPIRE IN 1935

USSR

OUTER
MONGOLIA

SAKHALIN
ISLAND

MANCHUKUO
(1932)

KARAFUTO
(1905)

INNER
MONGOLIA

KURIL
ISLANDS
(1875)

Mukden

Beijing

Liadong
Peninsula
(1905)   Port Arthur

Yellow

Seoul
KOREA
(1910)

Tokyo

CHINA

Pacific
Ocean

Nanjing

Yangzi

Shanghai

RYŪKYŪ ISLANDS
(1874)

Hong Kong

TAIWAN
(1895)

0   500 mi
0   500km

PHILIPPINE
ISLANDS

Asia, using the Anglo-Japanese Alliance as justification for taking over most of Germany's possessions in China and the Pacific. They also sent troops into Siberia near the end of the war, a disastrous move apparently aimed at establishing a buffer zone against the newly established Soviet Union.

Taishō foreign policy played out most vividly in Japan's colonies. By the early 1920s, the empire included Taiwan, Korea, Karafuto (secured in the Russo-Japanese War), and the Micronesian islands (taken from Germany, and then mandated to Japan as a trusteeship after World War I), in addition to semicolonial holdings in Manchuria. The colony that mattered most to the Japanese in these years was Korea, which was turned into a protectorate after the Russo-Japanese War and annexed in 1910. The ostensible goal was to bring "civilization" to Korea, and during the Taishō years the Japanese worked effectively to develop Korea's infrastructure, creating schools, building transportation networks, and improving agriculture. They also encouraged industries, paving the way for some Koreans to found lucrative businesses that later would grow into financial empires. However, Korean prosperity was never Japan's priority; above all, Japan sought to use Korea to improve its own economy and enhance its international standing, which meant that individual Koreans received few benefits. Indeed, tens of thousands of farm families had their land confiscated, and most new business permits were given to Japanese, not Koreans. As a result, Korean nationalists resisted forcefully, killing more than 7,000 Japanese during the first five years of control. And on March 1, 1919, more than a million demonstrators throughout the peninsula supported a declaration demanding "independence in the interest of the eternal and free development of our people."[12] Although the demonstrations drew international attention, they did not threaten Japan's standing in the world, since the other powers employed similar policies in their own colonies.

The Taishō emperor died in 1926. Over the next few years, as his son Hirohito matured in office as the Shōwa emperor, the country's mood changed. The social and intellectual energies of the Taishō years lost momentum; the government became even more intrusive; right-wing voices grew louder; and Japanese troops became more aggressive in Asia. The Taishō balance came apart. Why? Although no simple answers present themselves, one explanation clearly lies in the impact of unforeseen events. Three quite distinct episodes occurred at the turn of the decade, interacting in a way that, by the time they had run their course, left the country in a different place.

First came the Great Depression. Japan's economy, which had stagnated in the late 1920s, plummeted after the New York stock market crash in October 1929. Over the next several years, foreign firms cut back on their purchases of Japanese goods, and by 1931 the country's exports to the United States had dropped 40 percent, those to China 50 percent, and its GNP had fallen 18 percent. The personal costs were horrendous: more than a million unemployed workers, labor violence, soaring bankruptcies. Things were especially bad in rural regions where declining markets, along with crop failures in 1931 and 1934, took food from the table and made it impossible to pay rents. The protagonist in Mishima Yukio's novel *Runaway Horses* said of Japan's northwest in 1931: "Whatever could be sold was sold, land and homes were lost,...and people held starvation at bay by eating acorns and roots. Even in front of the township hall one saw notices such as: 'Anyone wishing to sell his daughters, inquire within.' "[13] The sense of vulnerability led people to seek scapegoats, which they found in party politicians who proved incapable of preventing the crisis and in foreign-oriented businesses that profited from the price fluctuations and changes in monetary policy. Many people began to question Japan's participation in an international system that rendered it susceptible to Western markets.

A second crisis was ignited by the 1930 London naval conference, which was held to update the 1922 Washington agreements. Japan's delegates went into the sessions hoping to improve their warship tonnage to 70 percent of that allowed the Americans and British. After intense discussions, however, they accepted an extension of Washington's five-five-three formula on large cruisers, with the desired 70 percent on small cruisers and a promise that the proposal would be revisited in five years. Back home, naval officials and the public expressed outrage over this capitulation, thinking that their diplomats had been outmaneuvered—and convinced that the international system was skewed against Japan. In November, a right-wing youth shot Prime Minister Hamaguchi Osachi, apparently out of anger over the London agreement; Hamaguchi died the following August.

If the depression and the naval conference inspired skepticism about the world system, an event in northeast China convinced millions that it was time for Japan to be more aggressive on the continent. Japan had expanded its activities in Manchuria steadily after winning that region in the Russo-Japanese War, and by 1930 Manchuria had become a colony in all but name. Using the South Manchuria Railway Company as their engine and the Manchuria-based Guandong (Kwantung) Army to enforce security, Japanese officials had developed a vast structure controlling more than 100 towns, the continent's most impressive railroad system, and a network of mines, power plants, ports, and farms. By 1930, a quarter of a million Japanese lived in Manchuria, and railway company revenues totaled 34 million yen annually.

As in Korea, the Japanese presence provoked local resistance, especially as battle-torn China became increasingly unified under Chiang Kai-shek in the late 1920s. Students staged boycotts, and workers struck Japanese firms, demanding withdrawal. By the late 1920s, Japanese officials were divided about how to respond. While many thought Japan should be more sensitive to Manchurian interests, others wanted firmer responses. The hand of the latter group was strengthened late in 1928 by the arrival in Port Arthur of Ishiwara Kanji, an army lieutenant colonel with his own plans for making Japan stronger. Convinced by his reading of apocalyptic Buddhist writings that Japan must prepare for an approaching "final war," Ishiwara led several officers in bombing a section of the South Manchuria Railway outside Mukden (Shenyang) on the night of September 18, 1931, and blaming it on Chinese activists. The damage was slight, but he achieved his purpose. While the Tokyo cabinet debated how to respond to China's "attack," Ishiwara's group created another incident north of Mukden, in the city of Jilin, to make Japanese residents there appear to be in danger. The Guandong Army then took over Jilin, and an irate cabinet, left with few options, approved the Manchurian moves. Thus began a series of episodes that would culminate in the creation of the state of Manchukuo on February 15, presided over nominally by China's last Manchu emperor, Pu Yi, and controlled by Japan. To citizens back home, long accustomed to bowing before Westerners, it appeared that Japan finally had stood up. Unilateralism was new—and it was popular.

Though the 1930s are often painted in a militarist monochrome, they actually were multihued. On the surface, public life continued much as it had before. Café society flourished. Magazines publicized scandals and successes, and the radio broadcast popular tunes, as the number of radios quintupled to five million. Professional baseball began in 1934, making a star of Sawamura Eiji, who struck out Babe Ruth during an exhibition game. Youthful materialism still worried traditionalists, but most people were more interested in the 1936 Berlin Olympics than in the traditionalists' rants. Despite several terrorist episodes, city streets remained safe, and normal legal procedures remained intact. When the courts found the defendants innocent in a 1937 stock-purchase scandal, they were showcasing their independence, defying both right-wing opinion and the Justice Ministry.

The economy, too, returned to normal. Government spending on public works and the military poured cash into the country, and the December 1931 decision to go off the gold standard made Japanese goods cheaper abroad and fueled foreign trade. By mid-decade, Japan's recovery had surpassed that of the United States and the Europeans. A number of new commercial giants emerged in the 1930s, among them the conglomerate Nissan and the Japan Nitrogen Fertilizer Company (Nichitsu). By the late 1930s, leading economists were talking about Japan's "economic miracle."[14] Political life also continued in generally healthy fashion, with elections won by the relatively liberal Minseitō in three of the decade's four Lower House elections. Political party heads no longer served as prime minister after 1932, but the parties themselves remained influential. Opposition voices rang out forcefully, to the end of the decade. In 1935, for example, the Nagoya journalist Kiryū Yūyū worried in his magazine *Stones from A Different Mountain* that militarism would lead Japan to war. "The thing we fear so greatly," he said, "is that the second world war will be more cruel, more inhuman, even than the first one.... It is conceivable that people in every civilized country will come to know the tragedy of death."[15]

Neither prosperity nor opposition essays, however, could mask the fact that society was changing significantly as the 1930s progressed. No one, for example, could miss the upsurge in hyperpatriotic rhetoric. Nationalist voices, an important submelody in Taishō, became dominant now. Old organizations such as the Black Sea Society and the Amur River Society demanded with new vigor that Japan be more active on the continent, and newer groups like the State Foundation Society sought to eradicate socialism and replace "the anti-nationalist political parties" with "the Emperor at the centre of political life."[16] Membership in these groups ran into the tens of thousands and included increasing numbers of officials and businessmen, almost all of whom demanded a "Shōwa Restoration": code for removing Western-oriented politicians, bureaucrats, and big businessmen from leadership, much as the Meiji Restoration had removed the Tokugawa "usurpers."

The influence of these groups was multiplied by increasing activism among right-wingers in the military and the government. In the army, two dozen young officers formed the secretive Sakurakai (Cherry Blossom Society) late in 1930 to counter a system in which "top leaders engage in immoral conduct" and "political parties are corrupt."[17] And in the government, the military maneuvered admirals and generals into the office of prime minister repeatedly after 1932. One of the rare nonmilitary prime ministers, Hirota Kōki, said the military became "like an untamed horse left to run wild.... The only hope is to jump on from the side and try to get it under control while still allowing it to have its head to a certain extent."[18] Rightist bureaucrats succeeded in 1937 in getting the Education Ministry to produce a school booklet called *Kokutai no hongi* (Cardinal principles of the national polity), which asserted that Japan was superior to other countries because of the divine lineage of its emperors.

Ultranationalism showed its most frightening face in the streets, where true believers sought to publicize their agenda through what today would be called acts of terrorism. On May 15, 1932, young naval officers, cooperating with the nationalist society League of Blood, assassinated prime minister Inukai Tsuyoshi, hoping to force the military to declare martial law and take over the government. They failed in that aim, but the assassination ended political party government, and the perpetrators' passionate courtroom defenses, given free rein by judges, inspired wide public sympathy. Similar acts followed in the mid-1930s. Then, on February 26, 1936, a larger incident forced a change in national policy. During a morning snowstorm, 1,400 members of the army's Imperial Way faction seized central Tokyo, assassinating three leading officials and demanding a Shōwa Restoration. They surrendered two days later in the face of a massive army crackdown, after the emperor raged against "these criminally brutal officers who killed my aged subjects who were my hands and feet" and threatened that if the army did not quell the rising quickly, "I will personally lead the Imperial Guard Division and subdue them."[19] The scale of the uprising shocked society and prompted a strong government response, which brought terrorism to an end. But nationalist fervor did not wane.

Indeed, it had become a matter of personal survival by the mid-1930s for citizens to make a show of their patriotism, to the point that even leading communists had begun announcing their conversion to nationalism. When Minobe was forced to resign his Diet seat in 1935 for defending his organ theory, many decided the price of resisting the tide had become too high. Novelists like Kawabata Yasunari, an eventual Nobel Prize winner, turned to traditional Japanese themes. Women's movement leaders like Ichikawa Fusae, known earlier as peace advocates, pushed for the inclusion of women in the nationalist program. Internationalists like Nitobe Inazō, disillusioned by Western colonial hypocrisy, became defenders of expansionism. In academia, too, nationalist ideologies triumphed. When Ienaga Saburō entered Tokyo University as a liberal-leaning graduate student in 1934, he found that "the whole atmosphere...had undergone a total change from what it had been before I arrived." Japanism, he said, made the history department "an awful place."[20]

Japan's colonial policies also were affected by the changing mood, as economic vitality replaced power and prestige as the prime goal. Shocked during the depression by the West's economic nationalism and the unreliability of international markets, which had sent Manchurian exports into a tailspin, Japan's leaders began talking about the need to make the empire self-sufficient economically. Independence from the Western powers; self-sufficiency within the empire; total Japanese dominance—these became the central goals.

The change was evident across the Tsushima Straits. The colonial government turned in a harsher direction in Korea in the 1930s; by decade's end, families were being forced to adopt Japanese surnames, and students were allowed to use only Japanese in the classroom. By 1940, three-fourths of Korea's capital investment was in Japanese hands. The movement toward a tightly controlled, Japan-oriented economy was clearer still in Manchuria, which now took central place in the empire. Administrative authority shifted away from the South Manchurian Railway Company to the Guandong Army, with its 270,000 troops. Japan poured almost six billion yen into the colony during the decade after 1932: building railway lines to nearly fifty new cities; constructing automobile, weapons, and farm equipment factories; and digging coal mines. As the 1940s began, more than 750,000 Japanese farmers were living in a thousand Manchurian towns and villages.

Not surprisingly, the new colonial policies spawned a growing sense of isolation from the Western powers, even as they pulled the military farther into north China. When the League of Nations condemned the creation of Manchukuo in February 1933, Japan left the League, giving a hollow ring to the emperor's assurance that Japan would not "isolate itself thereby from the fraternity of nations."[21] When 350,000 Chinese joined resistance units, officials began discussing the need for more troops and additional buffer zones around Manchukuo. Following fighting that spring in Hebei Province to the south, Japan pressured Chiang Kai-shek into signing the Tanggu Truce, which gave Japan control of the area east of Beijing and created a demilitarized zone between Beijing and the Great Wall. Then, moving still farther afield, the Guandong Army created its own north China regional government a year later, agreeing as compensation to help Chiang defend his Nationalist government against the communists.

All of these initiatives set the stage for a sharp increase in authoritarian, anti-Western domestic behavior after mid-decade. Moving away from free market policies, officials nationalized the electrical power industry in 1936, and then created a Cabinet Policy Bureau a year later to guide the economy. A ministers' conference in mid-1936 drew up a list of eventualities that might make it necessary to take control of all East Asia. In November, the government signaled its strategic drift by signing an Anti-Comintern Pact with Germany, agreeing to share information about the spread of Soviet communism. Scholars debate whether Japan turned fascist in the late 1930s; no one questions, however, that the military's influence had become dominant and that Japan was becoming increasingly isolated from its former allies.

The spark that turned all of China into an inferno was another incident, on July 7, 1937, when shots fired at Japanese troops on maneuvers southwest of Beijing led to skirmishes with local troops. As in 1931, an isolated incident expanded into something bigger. The immediate impetus this time was Chiang Kai-shek, who sent troops to Beijing in contravention of the Tanggu Truce and proclaimed with considerable bluster that he would allow no more Japanese expansion in northeast China. Tokyo countered with its own bravado, despite Ishiwara's warning that if Japan responded harshly, "we may...find ourselves with a full-scale war on our hands. The result would be the same sort of disaster which overtook Napoleon in Spain—a slow sinking into the deepest sort of bog."[22] By late July, the two countries were at war. Japan took Beijing, Shanghai, and Nanjing during the next six months, and eventually created its own puppet government in China. But things did not go well. It took three months of vicious fighting for Japan to win in Shanghai. Then in Nanjing, after an easier triumph, Japanese troops went on a seven-week rampage, raping and murdering 100,000—perhaps even 200,000—civilians in a barbaric massacre that would trouble East Asian relations for decades. And Chiang, rather than capitulating, moved his capital inland to Chongqing, where he mounted an ongoing resistance that rendered Japan's puppet government meaningless. The politicians and generals had predicted easy victory, but it was soon clear that Ishiwara was the prescient one.

Over the next few years, Japan experienced increasing frustration. Despite official promises of a prosperous "New Order for East Asia," Japanese troops were thwarted by communist fighters in China's north and Chiang's resistance in the central highlands. Making things worse, a combination of cunning, desperation, and racism led to barbarous acts by Japan's military—acts that most Japanese would have believed impossible—including the theft of farmers' land for food and the torture and killing of villagers. Most notorious, after the Nanjing massacre, was Unit 731, which conducted biological experiments on perhaps 3,000 Manchurians, injecting them with various diseases, including bubonic plague, in an effort to develop techniques in bacteriological warfare. Asked after the war to account for his willingness to take part in the experiments, one soldier blamed racism: "If we didn't have a feeling of racial superiority, we couldn't have done it." He added, "I have to say war is a dirty thing.... I am a war criminal."[23]

At home, existence became more regulated and more difficult after the General Mobilization Law of April 1938 gave the state the right to control nearly all areas of national life in a time of emergency. When an emergency was declared a month later, the government began taking steps to bring the economy wholly under its supervision, regulating prices and the flow of money, assigning workers to crucial industries, and providing assistance to favored businesses and institutions. A full three-quarters of government spending went to the military now. The press was monitored more rigorously. In 1940, the government replaced political parties with a single overarching organization, the Imperial Rule Assistance Association, intended to stifle disagreements. The justice minister told legislators: "This is a matter of wartime. Because this is a situation in which the nation must fight for victory or defeat, subjects tender all their strength and all their goods."[24]

Meanwhile, the rift with Western allies widened. A 1939 battle against the Soviets in the west Manchurian region of Nomonhan resulted in a drubbing, and 18,000 Japanese deaths. The estrangement from the United States was more gradual. The Americans renounced the bilateral commercial treaty in 1939 and then stopped selling aviation gas and scrap iron to Japan in 1940, in response to its continued aggression in China, as well as its growing ties with Germany and Italy. The two nations spent much of 1941 in negotiations, as Japan sought recognition of its Manchurian holdings while the United States demanded that the Japanese withdraw from all of China. After Japan invaded southern Indochina (a French colony) in July 1941, the United States froze Japan's American assets, but the talks continued, and Japan eventually offered to withdraw from Indochina, as well as from significant parts of China. When the Americans flatly rejected all of Japan's proposals, a late November liaison conference, held to coordinate the views of the cabinet and the military, set the final date for an attack on the United States. One of the conferees suggested that the decision be worded so "that there will be some room for negotiations"; the navy chief of staff replied, "There is no time for that."[25]

Japan bombed the U.S. naval forces at Pearl Harbor, Hawaii, on December 7, 1941, following an imperial declaration that "Our Empire for its existence and self-defense has no other recourse,"[26] and for several months the army devoured everything in its path, taking Hong Kong on December 25, Malaya and Singapore in February, the Dutch East Indies (Indonesia) in March, and Burma and the Philippines in May. One American general said, "We were out-shipped, out-planed, out-manned and out-gunned."[27] These successes were temporary, however. Japan's army remained mired in China, and after fighting to a near draw in the Battle of the Coral Sea off southern New Guinea in early May, Japan's navy suffered a crushing defeat by the Americans in the battle of Midway in June, losing nearly as many men as it had killed at Pearl Harbor. After that, the "holy war" turned defensive. A vicious fight for Guadalcanal, east of New Guinea, during the fall and winter of 1942–1943 resulted in heavy losses on both sides but a Japanese defeat. Over the next two years, the Allies took back all they had lost and more, island by island. By mid-1944, the Japanese were defending the last of their central Pacific islands in vicious encounters that killed most of the Japanese and up to three-fourths of the attackers. At Saipan, which was typical, nearly 95 percent of Japan's 43,000 troops were killed before the July surrender, and 4,000 civilians committed mass suicide.

Writers often refer to the homeland in these years as a "dark valley." While a semblance of normalcy marked daily life in the early months of the war, the mobilization was massive. Neighborhood associations dispensed information and sold war bonds. Middle school boys were drafted into war industries, twelve-year-old girls pressured to go to work alongside foreigners and war prisoners. Mass organizations were created to inculcate patriotism among workers, women, and farmers. Authorities punished nonconformist journalists by sending them off to the army. At the same time, the country's growing desperation became harder and harder to hide. By 1944, the economy was in complete shambles: hunger was endemic, worker absenteeism was soaring, and urbanites were fleeing in droves to the countryside. "Today I heard that the radish we grate for one meal now will be our vegetable allotment for three days," wrote a Tokyo housewife in January 1945. "What are we to do?"[28] Civilians were under direct military attack by late 1944, too, targets of Allied bombs that eventually wiped out a quarter of Japan's homes and left thirteen million homeless, witnesses to scenes such as that in Kyoto on March 10, 1945, when "corpses, arms, and legs were hanging from the electric wires; household goods were strewn on railroad tracks." "How," a billiards parlor owner asked in his diary, "could there be a living heart in all this?"[29]

Confronted by this spreading disaster, many officials had begun searching for ways to end the war by the spring of 1945, and they intensified their efforts after Okinawa fell in June, following a horrific battle that claimed perhaps 250,000 civilian and military lives. They were stalemated, however, by the army's old guard, which refused to stop fighting, at least until assured that the imperial institution would survive. It took the world's first atomic bombs, dropped by the United States on Hiroshima and Nagasaki on August 6 and 9, combined with the Soviets' July 8 declaration of war against Japan, to break the stalemate. Early firebombings had created nearly as much damage, but the 200,000 deaths this time had resulted from just two small weapons. And the human nightmares had been even more graphic. "I saw men and women all red, burned," a Korean resident of Hiroshima said. "Faces hung down like icicles.... You couldn't walk the streets without stepping over the dead."[30] That, plus fear of the Soviets, prompted the

The view from the Urakami branch of Nagasaki prison, about 300 meters from the hypocenter of the atomic bomb dropped by the United States on August 9, 1945. All 134 prisoners and workers were killed. Photo by H. J. Peterson. Courtesy of Nagasaki Atomic Bomb Museum.

emperor at last to speak up for surrender. On August 15, he announced in a scratchy radio recording that continuing the war "would lead to the total extinction of human civilization"; he had "ordered the acceptance of the provisions of the Joint Declaration of the Powers."[31]

Thus the war came to an end—leaving in its wake a host of issues that would stir debate and reflection for decades. There was, for example, the question of human depravity: the massacres carried out by Japanese troops, the experiments on living people, the brutal treatment of prisoners, the famine caused by cynical policies in Vietnam, and the conscription of at least 100,000 "comfort women," 80 percent of them Korean, to provide sex for Japanese troops. That other Allied and Axis nations had carried out similar atrocities simply underscored the questions raised by these behaviors. Another issue was the human cost of war. Nearly two million Japanese soldiers perished, and millions more Asians died at Japanese hands, perhaps fifteen million in China alone. Half a million Japanese died in Allied attacks on civilians; families across the continent were ripped apart. If the Japanese became pacifists after the war, it probably was due more to the pain inflicted by this carnage than to postwar policies. Finally, there was an ironic consequence: the end of colonialism. By driving the Europeans out of Southeast Asia during the war, Japan had changed local dynamics in ways that ended the viability of colonialism for the long term. Japan had begun the twentieth century in optimism and approached its midpoint in ashes. The colonies had experienced the reverse. Long oppressed, they greeted 1946 with hope, ready for freedom from their colonial masters.

A New Kind of Power
(after 1945)

When the Shōwa emperor opened the Tokyo Olympics on October 10, 1964, few missed the significance. Here was Japan's wartime sovereign, presiding over a gathering of 75,000 spectators and 5,000 athletes from ninety-four nations. The torch-lighter was a Waseda University runner born in Hiroshima the day the atomic bomb was dropped. When the games closed two weeks later, Japan had won a record sixteen gold medals, and journalists had rhapsodized about the country's reentry into the community of nations. Olympics president Avery Brundage declared Japan the "Olympic nation No. 1 in all the world."[1]

This triumph hinted in several ways at the contours of Japan's entire postwar era. On the surface, it dramatized the nation's success in restoring not just peace but economic vitality, and in doing so rapidly. At less obvious levels, it demonstrated the complexities underlying growth. Bureaucratic infighting over spending on the games' infrastructure, particularly over the cost of the world's first bullet train, called attention to domestic political struggles that would mark the whole era. The fact that the Americans won the most gold medals highlighted Japan's ongoing subordination to that enemy-turned-ally. The use of sports to woo the world exemplified an indirect approach to diplomacy that would evoke both admiration and criticism.

The Olympic triumph did not come easily. When the war ended, Japan was in ashes, with more than sixty-five cities bombed into what residents called *yaki nohara* (burned-out plains), nearly three million people dead, 60 percent of the country's factories out of operation, and a quarter of the nation's wealth eradicated. One teacher recalled looking in the washroom mirror that summer: "I gave a start. My own face had aged so much I didn't recognize it, and a sort of shadow of death appeared....In those days malnutrition caused changes in appearance, and lots of people looked ghastly." He recalled, too, how his emotionally exhausted relatives had "snarled at each other, clamored fiercely, seemed virtually to have gone mad."[2] For many, the hard times would continue for years, as obstacle followed obstacle. The year after the war ended, thirteen million—a full sixth of the population—remained unemployed. As late as 1949, homeless people were starving to death, and families were searching for hundreds of thousands of still unaccounted-for loved ones who had gone abroad during the expansionist decades.

These trials notwithstanding, Japan's return to health began almost as soon as the formal surrender documents were signed on September 2. The recovery process was overseen by the Occupation government, which operated formally under the supervision of the Allies but was run by the Americans, who came to Japan in great numbers in the fall of 1945. Known as the Supreme Commander of the Allied Powers (SCAP) and dominated by the towering, aloof Douglas MacArthur, the Occupation bureaucracy took charge with the audacity of a conqueror, aiming to restore Japan to economic health as a demilitarized, thoroughgoing democracy. In the words of one Japanese cartoonist who had seen American bombs fall from the wartime skies: "From the very same sky, the gift of peace began to descend. So-called democratic revolution!"[3]

A key feature of the Occupation was SCAP's decision to work through Japan's existing government. In contrast to Germany, where the Allies simply replaced the old government with their own, SCAP officials set up a two-pronged structure, with MacArthur's administration setting policies and providing oversight while the Japanese government ran day-to-day affairs. This approach led to bitter and frequent disputes, but the arrangement worked, because both sides harbored similar goals. SCAP officials had decided early on to create a strong, democratic ally rather than merely to punish Japan. The Japanese, exhausted by war, were determined to cooperate. Both wanted a strong, peaceful country. The one exception came in Okinawa, where the Americans set out, in contravention of Japanese desires, to create a tightly authoritarian occupation government, which they intended to maintain permanently.

In the early postwar months, progressive officials in both SCAP and the Japanese bureaucracy used the wide disillusionment with militarism to win support for many democratic initiatives. Reformers removed nationalistic materials from school textbooks; MacArthur encouraged labor unions and collective bargaining; writers and publishers won new freedoms; and massive land reforms transferred farm acreage from the landlords to the tillers. Most influential of all was a new constitution, which took effect in 1947. After rejecting a conservative Japanese revision of the Meiji constitution, MacArthur created his own committee of SCAP officials early in 1946, charged with drafting a document that would outlaw war, maintain the imperial institution, and foster equality. The committee worked feverishly, nights as well as days, and within a week had prepared an English-language draft that turned governance on its head, providing for a bicameral legislature, assuring equal rights for women (a point insisted on by committee member Bette Sirota, who had grown up in Japan), spelling out a broad range of civil liberties, and declaring that "all people have the right to maintain the minimum standards of wholesome and cultured living" (article 25). The most controversial stipulation was article 9, which stated that "the Japanese people forever renounce war as a sovereign right of the nation" and that "land, sea and air forces, as well as other war potential, will never be maintained."[4]

While these provisions gave Japan one of the world's most liberal constitutions, MacArthur's reason for supporting them was conservative: he wanted to preserve the emperor's status. Having concluded that the imperial institution was needed to assure stability, he had an aide

Japanese schools continued to hold classes following World War II, even when they had to meet outdoors, as did this Okinawan music class in the fall of 1945. National Archives, SC 210185.

tell a group of Japanese hard-liners: "The only possibility of retaining the Emperor and the remnants of their own power is by their acceptance and approval of a Constitution that will force a decisive swing to the left."[5] Thus, he supported a more progressive constitution than he was personally comfortable with. He also had the emperor in mind in structuring the other major antimilitary initiative, the Tokyo war crimes trials, which, like their counterpart trials in Nuremberg, were intended to bring to justice those most responsible for the war. When the tribunal convened in May 1946, Hirohito was not among the twenty-five men charged with "crimes against humanity" and "crimes against peace." Standing against a chorus of demands that the emperor be tried, Mac-Arthur argued that his indictment would "cause a tremendous convulsion among the Japanese people.... Destroy him and the nation will disintegrate."[6] The result was a trial in which references to the imperial family and to Japan's war crimes in China were largely omitted. By November 1948, when all twenty-five were found guilty (seven received death sentences), the trials' goal of teaching the Japanese lessons about militarism had been undermined by a weary public's conclusion that the verdicts were little more than "victor's justice."

Before eighteen months had passed, SCAP officials were thinking less about democratizing Japan than about restoring stability. Worried by rising communism in Europe and China, as well as by Japan's continuing economic woes, MacArthur decided that America and Europe needed a strong Asian ally more than a democratic model. He exhibited this new attitude at the end of January 1947, when he prohibited a general strike that had been planned to protest low wages. Union leaders and leftists felt betrayed, and the head of the strike's organizing committee shouted at Occupation officials, "Japanese workers are not American slaves!" before backing down.[7] Conservatives rejoiced, however. The next years would see similar shifts in many spheres, including the SCAP-supported creation of a 75,000-man National Police Reserve, supposedly intended to augment local police forces but equipped with army-style machine guns and tanks. The new policies also resulted in a government-led purge, early in the 1950s, of 13,000 alleged communists from jobs in the press, radio, labor, and the film industry, and the closure of nearly 1,500 leftist papers and journals.

This reverse course had a particularly strong impact on economic policies. Occupation officials began having second thoughts about their determination to crush the engines of the wartime economy when it became clear that ordinary measures were not solving the massive problems. In the third year after the war, the annual inflation percentage still soared above 200, and production stood at 37 percent of prewar levels. For individual citizens, this meant endless scavenging for food, homeless people dying of exposure in the winter months, and black markets still charging five times the official price rates in 1948. Almost everyone had to skirt the law in one way or another to secure food for the table, prompting one editorialist to quip, "In today's Japan, the only people who are not living illegally are those in jail."[8]

One result of the continuing difficulties was that SCAP officials began to reconsider their plans for demolishing the prewar cartels known as *zaibatsu* (economic cliques), on the grounds that a healthy nation needed large business organizations. In the end, they broke up just eleven large companies instead of the 300 originally intended. Another was the decision in 1949 to bring in banker Joseph Dodge as an economic czar to set things right. Unfortunately, his stern policies initially did more damage than good. When he cut government assistance to the private sector and insisted that already hard-pressed ministries cut their budgets, the economy went into a further tailspin; industry found itself increasingly desperate for capital, and the stock market fell, while unemployment and bankruptcies rose. Whether his policies would have led to eventual recovery is uncertain. What is clear is that it took an unanticipated development—the coming of the Korean War in June 1950—to finally turn the economy around. As that war progressed, Japan became a huge supply center, and the economy began to take off. Prime Minister Yoshida Shigeru referred to the conflict as a divine gift.

The Occupation came to an end on April 28, 1952, as a result of a forty-eight-nation peace treaty signed in San Francisco the previous September. Once again, Japan was a sovereign country, free to pursue its own course. The man who presided over the transition into self-rule was the autocratic Yoshida, who as prime minister had been MacArthur's counterpoint for all but seventeen months of the Occupation after May 1946. A part of the old conservative establishment, Yoshida preferred results over ideology—a fact made particularly clear in his approach to armaments. Despite American pressure late in the Occupation for Japan to rearm (article 9 notwithstanding), he had insisted forcefully that Japan should take a "go-slow" approach to arms, maintaining only a small force. Similarly, in the field of foreign affairs, he argued that his country's postwar future lay with the United States, even though he would have preferred close ties to Great Britain. "This is not essentially a question of either dogma or philosophy," he said. "It is merely the quickest and most effective way—indeed the only way—to promote the prosperity of the Japanese people."⁹ The three pillars of his national policy—disarmament, trade, Japanese-American cooperation—came over time to be labeled the Yoshida Doctrine.

The foundation of the bilateral relationship was the 1951 Japan-U.S. Security Treaty, which allowed the Americans to maintain military bases in Japan (nearly 3,000 of them at the time) in return for assisting Japan with security. In practice, the treaty had two primary effects. It meant that Japan would be able to remain lightly armed, in keeping with Yoshida's policies, spending a mere 1 percent of its GNP on the military. And it assured a uniquely close relationship between the two Pacific powers. The treaty touched off endless debates, as well as frequent demonstrations by those who resented the fact that in signing it Japan had given up diplomatic and military autonomy. Protests occurred regularly at military bases, and more than thirty million citizens signed antinuclear petitions after the United States' 1954 hydrogen bomb tests at Bikini atoll killed a crewman on the Japanese fishing vessel *Lucky Dragon*. In 1960, when the security treaty was revised, nationwide anti-treaty protests toppled the government, even though the new treaty made the relationship more nearly equal, providing, among other things, that the United States would pay a larger share of the bases' cost and would give notice before bringing nuclear weapons onto Japanese soil. Nonetheless, the relationship was to provide a long-term linchpin for Japan's foreign policy, freeing the economy from the burdens of heavy military spending.

Yoshida's other major political achievement was to solidify conservative control of the government. The 1947 constitution may have created a progressive framework, but the conservative parties had taken charge once the Occupation's reverse course was in effect, and after 1952, they won a succession of elections with strong majorities. The post-Occupation Diets also passed several bills designed to strengthen the established parties' hold on power: one of them nationalized the police system, another banned activities likely to lead to violence (a throwback, many feared, to prewar authoritarianism). These bills made One-Man Yoshida, as he was called, unpopular, but he rammed them through. Although he lost a no-confidence vote in 1954 after calling a Diet member a "damned fool," he gave the conservatives an unassailable grip on power. Once the Liberal Democratic Party was formed in 1955 from the merger of the two leading conservative parties, it held office for thirty-eight straight years.

The happiest story of the 1950s surely was the resurgence of the economy. Fueled by favorable international trade policies and the ready availability of the latest Western technologies, as well as the daring and vision of entrepreneurs like Sony's Morita Akio and National Panasonic's Matsushita Kōnosuke, Japan's electronic and automotive industries mushroomed. Its exports soared. The economy grew at an annual rate of nearly 10 percent in the decade after the Occupation. As a result, people began accumulating money again—and using it to fuel a consumer explosion. Journalists drew on an ancient symbol, the "three imperial treasures," to talk about the country's "three electronic treasures": the washing machine, refrigerator, and television. Baseball regained its prewar popularity; fads included everything from hula hoops to embraceable little dolls called *dakkochan*; new cabarets and bars dotted old neighborhoods; and a fresh medium, the weekly general-interest magazine, attracted millions of subscribers with gossip and glossy photographs. Life improved even in the countryside, where rising rice prices, mechanization, and new insecticides allowed farmers to begin narrowing the income gap between themselves and their urban cousins.

This new consumerism was symbolized by the contrasting experiences of two women named Michiko. The first was Shōda Michiko, the wealthy businessman's daughter who met Crown Prince Akihito on a tennis court and then married him, becoming the first commoner ever to marry an emperor-to-be. Three million people bought TV sets to watch the couple's April 1959 wedding, and many more millions bought popular magazines to follow their story. "The Cinderella story of someone climbing upward has become a popular tale," one commentator wrote, "but the fact that in this case the imperial family moved downward, this is the true secret of this couple's popularity, and that is something I do not want to see forgotten."[10] The second, who drew nearly as much attention, was Kamba Michiko, a middle-class participant in the anti–security treaty movement. When she was killed in a 1960 demonstration, the new magazines produced an array of shamelessly sentimental articles, weeping over her death and playing on old gender types with articles about "the innocent eyes of...a sweet girl in a sailor-collared high school uniform" who should have had "a bright and beautiful future of romance, marriage, and childrearing."[11] Both episodes tied consumerism and politics together in a way that that would have been unthinkable in the Taishō years, when Japan had experienced its last consumer boom.

Consumerism also had a darker side, in the spread of what many described as an inner malaise. As money became available and memories of the war faded, some people pursued material possessions—and pleasures—with an abandon that recalled the 1920s, while others felt spiritually adrift in a culture without transcendent goals. Commentators wrote juicily, sometimes angrily, in the late 1950s about hedonists who wallowed in money-making and dissipation, greed-mongers typified by a University of Tokyo law student who founded a usurious lending club and wrote in his diary "To do business by making cunning use of others is a clear principle of economics."[12] Novelists deplored the emptiness of urban life: Niki Jumpei in Abe Kōbō's *Woman in the Dunes* sighs, after reading a set of dark newspaper headlines, "Everyday life was exactly like the headlines.... Everybody, knowing the meaninglessness of existence, sets the center of his compass at his own home."[13] Scholars probed the motives of millions of spiritual seekers who joined the "rush hour of the gods,"[14] attaching themselves to new religions that promised prosperity along with emotional succor. The largest of these, the lay organization of Nichiren Buddhism, called Sōka Gakkai, would use its ten million members to form a major political party, Kōmeitō, in the 1960s.

Neither malaise nor protests could slow down Japan's economic momentum, however, and the 1960s saw the country prosper as never before. Ikeda Hayato, prime minister from 1960 to 1964, was dubbed the "income-doubling" politician for his promise to increase Japan's GNP by 100 percent within a decade. Hardly a populist, he was a member of the Liberal Democratic Party economic elite, known for the quip "Let the poor eat barley." But the economy kept growing, and by mid-decade his promise had proved conservative. A combination of factors— a healthy climate for small businesses, Japanese workers' propensity for industriousness and high savings, the government's use of foreign exchange reserves to assist promising companies, low worldwide tariffs that encouraged trade—produced annual growth rates of more than 12 percent across the decade. By 1968, Japan had passed Germany to become the world's third largest economy, after the United States and the Soviet Union. By the end of the 1960s, it was dominating the world in sales of steel, aluminum, radios, television sets, pianos, automobiles, motorcycles, large ships, and cameras, among other products. Meanwhile, white-collar workers, called *sararīman* (salarymen), were leading a full-blown consumer revolution. In the countryside, where household income increased by nearly 60 percent across the decade, once-poor farmers were purchasing the same cars and TV sets as their city relatives. One farmer told a visiting scholar: "When we were children it was just straw sandals.... Children are expensive nowadays. The boys all want bicycles to go to school, and nothing less than one of those five-gear models will do."[15]

Prosperity was not enough, however, to make the feel-good quality of the early 1960s last; as the decade passed, it became increasingly clear that wealth carried its own problems. For one thing, high growth drew the critics' attention to Japan's timidity on the international stage, where the U.S. alliance kept the country from developing a strong profile of its own. More serious was a series of growth-related domestic difficulties. Urbanization, for example, was taking place too rapidly for the infrastructure to keep up. When the urban corridor from Tokyo to Osaka grew by nearly a third—to almost 50 million people—in the decade before 1965, housing construction lagged and land prices soared to almost thirty times what they were in the United States. The result was exorbitant rents for tiny apartments in huge complexes without adequate plumbing or efficient heating. The transportation system was overused, too: millions jammed onto rush-hour trains every morning, where pushers shoved as many bodies as possible into each car. "I try to count the number of passengers between us and the door," said a rider on the morning of a labor slowdown. "There are too many....It's difficult to step without treading on someone."[16]

High growth also damaged the environment, as mushrooming industries spewed out pollution. By the late 1960s, people were suffering an array of related afflictions, from stinging eyes and asthma to cadmium and mercury poisoning. In the most publicized case, refuse discharged by the Chisso chemical company into the poster-beautiful waters of Kyushu's Minamata Bay afflicted more than 10,000 residents with mercury poisoning, producing a wide range of crippling and disfiguring disabilities. One victim, the fisherman Hamamoto Sōhachi, insisted on going to work one morning despite being unable to speak clearly or walk steadily. When his boat rocked, he fell out, and stammered to his neighbor, "I've...got...that...strange...disease...that's going...around." He began shaking with convulsions—and died seven weeks later.[17] Such cases prompted a wave of lawsuits. They also gave rise to thousands of "citizens movements," in which town or neighborhood residents organized to fight local polluters—or nuclear weapons, or price gouging, or whatever the key local issue was. Led as often by newly politicized women as by men, these groups energized Japan's political scene in the early 1970s, pushing major antipollution legislation through the Diet and helping to elect progressive mayors in several cities.

Another wave of protests came from university students, stirred up by a mélange of issues, ranging from hostility toward U.S. involvement in the war in Vietnam to anger over poor teaching and rising university fees. They took to the streets and campus squares in great numbers in the late 1960s with attention-grabbing snake-dances, demonstrations, and strikes violent enough to shut down more than seventy universities. The most dramatic episode occurred at the University of Tokyo's Yasuda Hall in January 1969, when police and students fought violently for ten hours. The police won, and left Yasuda a charred hull. Smaller groups of students joined the protests of the right-wing novelist Mishima Yukio, who created his own Shield Society to arouse the public against the loss of Japan's martial vigor, a spiritual malady that was exemplified, he said, in the pacifist constitution and the security treaty. When an American agreement late in 1969 to return Okinawa to Japan sapped energy from the anti-treaty movement, Mishima concluded that his chances of inspiring mass actions were gone. Despondent, he went to the Army Self Defense Force headquarters in November 1970 and, after a bitter speech about Japan's spiritual emptiness, disemboweled himself in the ancient samurai ritual of *seppuku*—an act that riveted the media-immersed public but won few sympathizers.

Whereas the cheering winds of prosperity spawned a storm of growth-related problems in the 1960s, the next two decades reversed the pattern, as difficulties that preoccupied the public early on gave way to what many considered a golden age, at least economically. Citizen activism continued for a time over issues such as pollution and the location of Tokyo's new international airport. The fact that American military bases continued to occupy a full fifth of Okinawa's land space, even after the prefecture was returned to Japanese control, drew continuing opposition too. But the biggest issues of the early 1970s sprang from several episodes abroad that raised questions about Japan's role in the world and threatened its economic health. First came U.S. president Richard Nixon's announcement in July 1971 that he would go to China, thereby ending two decades of Sino-American estrangement. Most Japanese approved, but they were stunned that Nixon had not consulted them, given Japan's age-old closeness to China. Nixon also took two other steps that hurt Japan. He ended the long-term policy of holding the yen-to-dollar exchange rate at 360 to 1, causing the yen to rise against the dollar and making it harder to sell Japanese products in the United States. Then, in an effort to control food prices, he announced an embargo on the export of one of the products Japan needed most from the United States, soybeans. The embargo did not last long, but it enraged the Japanese people, who spoke derisively about the "Nixon shocks." An even more serious blow came from the Middle East in the fall of 1973, when the major oil-producing countries tripled prices and cut supplies by 30 percent. Lacking oil of its own, Japan was rocked by this move. Within a year, annual inflation had reached 25 percent and the GNP had declined by 1.4 percent. "This is the beginning of the New Price Revolution, a fundamental change in the price structure of commodities," one economist commented. The path ahead, he said, "is circumscribed by difficulties unknown—indeed never even imagined—in the 1960s."[18]

These difficulties produced Great Depression–style discussions of whether reliance on the international economy was in Japan's best interest, but the prevailing analysis was different this time. Rather than turning inward, the Japanese confronted the problems head on. They maintained their close ties to the United States but nurtured friendlier relationships with Arab countries to assure the flow of oil. Officials also cajoled labor into taking smaller wage increases and launched a raft of energy-related policies: encouraging conservation, developing non-oil energy sources, and promoting the energy-efficient automobiles that eventually would dominate Western markets.

As a result, the economy regained a solid footing relatively quickly, and annual growth rates of about 5 percent resumed. While the political sphere experienced tumult in the 1970s, with one prime minister driven from office by financial scandals and his four successors limited to short terms, Japan's economy had recovered sufficiently by 1978 to move through a second world oil shortage quite smoothly. At the decade's end, Japan had a $10 billion annual balance-of-payments surplus with the United States, and its per capita GNP had passed that of the Americans. The Harvard sociologist Ezra Vogel noted in a 1979 bestseller titled *Japan As Number One* that "Japanese institutions are coping with the same problems we confront, more successfully than we are."[19]

The 1980s seemed to confirm Vogel's appraisal. The country was awash in capital, and people were full of confidence. Already in the 1970s, essayists had begun churning out analyses of what made the Japanese special: their rice-growing roots, their language, their work ethic. Now their analyses took on a name—*Nihonjinron* ("on being Japanese")—and filled the bestseller lists. If many of these discussions appear ethnocentric or superficial today, Japan's economic dominance gave them credibility at the time. Organized around giant companies such as Toyota and Honda, and guided by general trading firms like Mitsubishi and Mitsui, Japan's economic energy seemed unstoppable.

By 1983, two of the world's four largest automakers were Japanese; by 1987, Japan's annual trade surplus exceeded $60 billion; in 1988, it had the world's ten largest banks, and at the decade's end, firms like Sony and National Panasonic were purchasing such American icons as CBS Records and Pebble Beach Golf Course. All the while, domestic land prices soared, and so did Tokyo's stock exchange.

This wealth produced a massive middle class in the 1980s, rooted in a competitive education system and bound together by the world's most advanced transportation network. The hardworking, company-oriented salaryman was still the urban norm, the one who held up Japan's economy and secured its values. He had studied hard in school (and in cram-school classes during evenings and weekends), negotiated his way through a hellish exam system to get into a good university, and then enjoyed his friends and ignored his studies at college. As an adult, he gave his life to a company, which provided him with lifetime employment, good wages, and steady promotions in return for his loyalty. He worked long hours, spent evenings drinking with colleagues, and paid outlandish fees to play golf on the weekend. All the while, his wife reared the children, readied them for those demanding entrance exams, and managed the family finances—including the husband's salary, which he turned over to her in exchange for a personal allowance. Like him, she socialized primarily with friends of her own gender. Together, they filled their home with all of the latest appliances. The solid, affluent nature of this life was captured by the businessman Arai Shinya in his 1986 novel *Shoshaman* (Company-man), which depicted his fellow workers' lives as secure but stifling. "Rare is the salaryman who has never agonized over his own impulse to quit the company," he said. "But in the end they beat their usual path to the drinking holes, where they mourn the death of their short-lived dreams and pour out their hearts in criticism of their immediate superiors."[20]

That this description approximated reality for millions of urbanites is beyond question. It was not, however, the whole reality. Millions of others lived less secure, less stereotypical lives: as poorly paid employees in the small firms that made up the lower tiers of Japan's business world; as grocery store clerks in family-owned shops; as hostesses and entertainers in the cities' ubiquitous bars and cabarets. There were also more than a few rebels, who refused to follow society's prescribed rules, regardless of their incomes or social backgrounds. By the early 1980s, social commentators had coined the word *shinjinrui* (new species) to depict a postwar social group that was unapologetic about pursuing personal satisfaction, even if that meant refusing to marry, for women, or quitting the company, for men. One of the *shinjinrui*, a hostess in a Sapporo bar, criticized the salaryman's preoccupation with creating social networks. "That is what old people do. I suppose it is very Japanese—I do it too, for business," she told an interviewer. "I do not think it is bad, it just takes a lot of time and effort, and... I would rather do other things."[21] She said she had no friends in the neighborhood where she lived. The cities also served as home to hundreds of thousands of true outsiders: the motorcycle gang members, unemployed rock musicians, drug users, and idlers who provoked establishment angst even as their self-indulgent lifestyles dramatized the country's affluence.

Affluence greatly influenced Japan's international standing in the 1980s. While domestic politics still took a backseat to economics, Japan's world presence grew rapidly. Its businessmen, of course, became a common sight in the world's major cities, and entrepreneurs like Sony's Morita and Honda Motor Company's Honda Sōichirō were known across the business world. But their presence was political, too. One reason was that Nakasone Yasuhiro, prime minister from 1982 to 1987, took an active approach to world affairs, boasting a first-name relationship with U.S. president Ronald Reagan and promoting "internationalization." He also pushed, though unsuccessfully, for a sharp increase in Japan's defense spending. Particularly noteworthy was Japan's increased engagement with Asia through participation in organizations like the Association of Southeast Asian Nations and the Peace Corps–like Overseas Cooperation Volunteers, which sent Japanese to do benevolent work in more than fifty countries. Japan also became the world's largest foreign aid donor in the late 1980s, giving out more than $10 billion a year.

This new international prominence, unfortunately, had a downside, subjecting Japan to increasing levels of criticism. Success itself prompted some of the attacks. In the United States, for example, where Japanese industries threatened everything from textiles to automobiles, public figures bashed Japan over allegedly unfair trade practices. One Midwestern auto dealer ran a full-page ad in his local newspaper declaring ominously that after "Japanese Zero's & Mitsubishi Bombers" threatened the Allies in World War II, "American planes blew them from the sky!"[22] In 1987, a congressman smashed a Toshiba radio in front of the Capitol. Other criticism was self-inflicted, instigated by Japan's insensitivity toward its neighbors. In 1985, when Nakasone made an official visit to Yasukuni, the shrine to Japan's war dead (including those convicted of war crimes), Asian governments protested vigorously. Similar protests arose when the education ministry revised history textbooks to soften descriptions of Japanese colonialism and wartime atrocities. Several politicians' expressions of racist opinions, including Nakasone's 1983 declaration that "the Japanese have been doing well for as long as 2,000 years because there are no foreign races,"[23] also drew fire. Economic might had made Japan visible, in ways once unimagined, and the results were often uncomfortable.

The Shōwa emperor's death early in 1989 after sixty-two years on the throne highlighted many of the contradictions of the decade—indeed, of the whole postwar era. Public discussion during his months-long death watch illustrated the continuing divide between a conservative establishment and progressives, who were still fighting for individual freedoms and human rights. While the former insisted on public displays of sympathy for the ailing emperor, the latter used the time to highlight continuing social injustices—even to raise questions about the emperor's wartime role. After Mayor Motoshima Hitoshi told the Nagasaki city assembly in December that the emperor should be held partially responsible for the war, a fierce controversy ensued, and a year later a right-wing extremist tried to assassinate him. When the emperor actually died on January 7, the middle class showed where its heart really lay by turning off the endless TV programs about the emperor and flocking to video stores, where they emptied the shelves of popular movies. The era's contradictions were on display at the funeral, too, when 163 nations sent representatives to mourn the man in whose name the Pacific War had been fought. The name chosen for his successor Akihito's reign was Heisei: "Establishing Peace."

One thing the emperor's death did not suggest, except to an insightful few, was how sharply Japan was about to change. If Hirohito's last decade had been filled with economic success, Heisei's first ten years proved the prescience of those Buddhist ancestors who pronounced all things fleeting. By 1990, the economy-that-could-do-no-wrong was in obvious trouble. The opening blow came when the stock market began to drop after the government tightened credit to curb speculative borrowing, and the Nikkei index plummeted from its December 1989 peak of nearly 39,000 to just over 14,000 in August 1992. That plunge highlighted a series of other economic problems, including the binge of earlier speculation that had led to inflated property values and a massive number of poorly secured loans. Consumer confidence went into a tailspin, and the country fell into a decade of economic woes, with rising unemployment, a drop in industrial production, weak consumer spending, and the collapse of numerous banks and stores. The GDP grew at

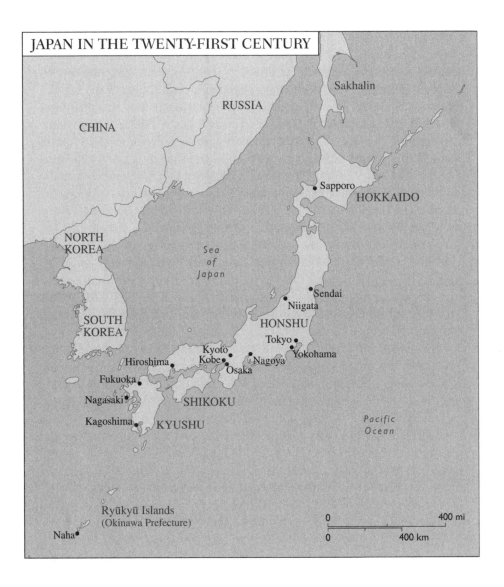

an average annual rate of less than 1 percent between 1992 and 1997, and in 1998 it actually declined. The economist Nariai Osamu captured the depth of the pessimism at the decade's end with his observation that "unless Japan can break through the present economic ceiling, it will find it difficult to achieve an industrial renaissance in the coming century."[24]

The economic typhoon betokened political difficulties, too. Domestically, prime ministers went through a revolving door; nine men served between 1989 and 1999, and several of them were driven from office by scandals. The most noteworthy was Murayama Tomiichi, who in 1994 became the first socialist prime minister since the Occupation. To survive, however, he had to cobble together a coalition with the Liberal Democratic Party, and when he left office two years later, his party was in shambles. The strongest prime minister was a Liberal Democratic Party old-timer, Hashimoto Ryutarō, who ruled without coalition partners from 1996 to 1998, but was forced to resign by a voter rebellion over a sales tax increase. The travails of the political sphere were symbolized by the government's bumbling response to the Great Hanshin Earthquake, which took more than 6,000 lives in the Kobe region early in 1995. "The Kobe earthquake not only destroyed a major city," a commentator wrote in the journal *Chūō Kōron*. "It also wrecked the nation's confidence in the central government's ability to cope with crises."[25] Two of the few bright spots in the quake's aftermath were the massive outpouring of citizen relief efforts and the first widespread use of electronic bulletin boards to spread information and coordinate operations.

Internationally, the situation was not much better, as economic woes bred disaffection. Japan remained actively engaged in the world, contributing $13 billion to America's effort in the Gulf War and sending the political scientist Ogata Sadako to the United Nations as the first female High Commissioner for Refugees. Japan also dispatched its Self Defense Forces to both hemispheres, as part of United Nations peacekeeping operations. But many of Japan's activities stirred controversy. In Okinawa, for example, the American bases—both the land they consumed and crimes committed by servicemen—created new tensions with the United States and fueled domestic protests. Japan was widely attacked for refusing to deal directly with the demands of the World War II "comfort women," even after the government admitted, early in the 1990s, that tens of thousands had been coerced into sex work. And critics across Asia hammered at Japan's failure to apologize officially for World War II, despite expressions of regret by several prime ministers and the emperor's personal apology to the Koreans in 1990. When the Diet's Lower House offered "sincere condolences" in June 1995 "to those who fell in action and victims of wars and similar actions all over the world," the statement's vague tone triggered even sharper criticism.[26]

The most complex, even baffling, feature of the 1990s was probably the impact the hard times had on the lives of average citizens. Press reports hewed to a standard line: Japan was going through another dark valley. A 1995 gas attack on the Tokyo subway system by the fringe religious group Aum Shinrykyō (Supreme Truth), which took twelve lives, was interpreted as evidence of widespread spiritual disaffection. The media wrote with relish about rootless youth—both students who bullied peers and graduates who lived off their parents rather than marrying or taking work—and about rising consumer debts and homelessness. They discussed the aging of Japan's population, as couples decided not to have children, old folks lived longer, and economists predicted that the economy could not support a nation in which the elderly might make up 40 percent of the population by the mid-2000s. Editorialists also discussed the 600 percent increase in government spending on the elderly during the 1990s, fretfully describing the Tokyo father who lamented, "When we were young, it seemed as if there were kids all over. Now it seems as if there are only elderly people like me."[27]

The problem with those accounts is not that they were inaccurate but that they were incomplete. For all the hand-wringing, daily life never lost its vitality for most Japanese. As an investment broker said of his countrymen: "They watch the Nikkei average every day as it drops, but it's like—you know the Japanese expression 'observing a fire on the other side of the river.'"[28] Consumers still spent their yen; world-renowned architects built stunning structures; savings and education levels remained high; popular culture was vibrant. In 1993, well after the recession had hit, foreign travel was ten times what it had been a decade earlier, and the American retailer L. L. Bean saw its Japanese sales soar. Something of the confidence and pride that remained in these years showed up in the forty million Japanese baseball fans who watched their compatriot Nomo Hideo pitch in America's 1995 All-Star Game. After watching that game, the historian Ikei Masaru wrote: "Americans...have many positive images of Japan and the Japanese. The Japanese are thought to be highly responsible and hard-working and to live in a relatively crime-free society, where a woman can walk home alone late at night. Educational standards are high, public hygiene is sound, and life expectancies are among the world's longest."[29] So much for the nation's pervasive gloom.

The 1990s' social energy may have been most apparent in family life, where people increasingly embraced the right to pursue personal satisfaction. By 2000, nuclear families were universal, love marriages nearly so. More and more husbands were coming home for dinner and helping with child rearing. On weekends, shopping centers overflowed with families and with couples walking hand in hand. Nonmarital options increased, too; many women put off marriage (or rejected

The residence of Kyushu architect Hamura Shoei Yoh overlooks the beach where Mongols invaded Japan in the late 1200s. His work is known for blending man-made structures with natural settings. In this home, says Hamura, "we have been learning the extreme beauty and awful phenomena" of nature. He has named the residence "Another Glass House between Sea and Sky." Courtesy of Hamura Shoei Yoh.

it altogether), and divorce rates rose to about half what they were in England and America. More women were pursuing careers outside the home. Indeed, by the decade's end, more women worked full-time out of than in the home. The middle-class affirmation of the "good life" surely is one reason that *A Healing Family*, the 1995 memoir by Nobel prize–winning novelist Ōe Kenzaburō, became a bestseller. Writing with stark frankness about family life with his autistic, epileptic son Hikari, he describes family meals, bouts of anger, sibling quarrels, hospital visits, the soothing power of music, and panic when Hikari gets lost. He envisions "how we...would have turned out if we hadn't made Hikari an indispensable part of our family": "I imagine a cheerless house where cold drafts blow through the gaps left by his absence."[30]

Signs of restored national health abounded in many spheres as the new millennium began. On the political front, Prime Minister Koizumi Jun'ichirō's five-year term (2001–2006) restored some stability and considerable energy to the government. Despite a confrontational approach that included six visits to Yasukuni and deployment of the Self Defense Forces to a conflict zone—Iraq—for the first time, his popularity remained high, particularly after he privatized the powerful postal system in 2005. His open-collared shirts and much-trumpeted admiration for Elvis Presley brought color to a drab world. And the economy began to recover. Even in the depression years, Japan had maintained solid fundamentals, with high savings rates, a relatively equitable distribution of wealth among classes, a strong yen, heavy government spending on public works, and large foreign reserves. Expanded exports (especially to China) and heavy investment now combined with consumer confidence to produce an economic expansion that, by 2006, would be the longest in postwar history. The rise of Internet firms was particularly impressive. Nearly 1,000 start-up companies went public in the decade before 2002, many of them reflecting the entrepreneurial spirit of Namba Tomoko, a young woman who founded the Internet auction company DeNA in 1999 and had a staff of seventy by 2003. "I was tired of designing businesses at a desk for someone else," she said. "There is nothing stopping a woman in striking out on her own in Japan anymore except her upbringing."[31]

Japan of the early twenty-first century was a technological paradise. Nowhere on earth was cell phone technology more advanced; nowhere did text messaging tie citizens together more fully. By 2008, Japan had more than eighty million cell phone Internet subscribers. Transportation systems were among the world's most advanced, too, with people tracking routes on GPS systems and watching the news overhead on commuter train monitors, even as they read novels on their cell phones. By the end of the decade, the Japanese were selling robotic suits that enabled disabled people to move more easily and reading food labels that gave environmental footprints. They had Asia's second highest per capita GDP, after Singapore, and the lowest inflation rate of any developed nation. And popular culture had absorbed the information revolution seamlessly, as sales of digital musical downloads rivaled those of CDs and DVDs.

Indeed, the sphere that integrated East and West most impressively in the early twenty-first century may have been popular culture. Western visitors typically commented on the prominence of Western things in Japan: Hollywood films, French fashions, British rock and soccer stars. But that was only half the story. By the early 2000s, Japan's cultural industry was truly international. It was dominated by home-grown groups and fads, and its influence abroad was immense. The cooking shows and reality programs on Japanese television were replicated on

American TV screens. Karaoke and instant ramen had become so common in the West that they were hardly thought of as Japanese, as had Power Rangers, Sudoku, and Transformers. Sushi was sold in small-town American supermarkets; Issey Miyake's fashion designs charmed Parisians; translations of *manga* (comic books) lined the shelves of bookstores around the globe; and Japanese baseball players starred in the U.S. major leagues. Most influential of all, surely, was *anime*, which made Miyazaki Hayao's Tottoro a world figure and inspired animation-viewing clubs across Europe and America. If Kurosawa Akira's *Rashomon* had drawn millions of moviegoers, Miyazaki's *Spirited Away* attracted tens of millions.

The challenges facing Japan early in the twenty-first century remained daunting. China's rising economic might, combined with resentments over World War II, made the threat of conflict serious. Interactions with North Korea, with its expanding missile program, were chilly—and potentially dangerous. Territorial disputes over fishing waters and resource-rich islands bedeviled relations with South Korea and China. At home, the 2008–2009 world financial crisis sent Japan's economy into a new downturn, and political scandals seemed endemic. There were also endless debates about Japan's role in the world, particularly whether it should reduce ties with the United States and amend the constitution to allow Japan to become a "normal" nation in its defense policies. Planners continued to worry about global warming and population decline too. Few questioned, however, the underlying dynamism, or fundamental stability, of Japanese society. Indeed, when voters turned the LDP out of power and sent a record fifty-four women to the Diet's Lower House in the fall of 2009, just as the economy had begun to recover from the financial crisis, many saw fresh evidence of the country's deep-seated, democratic vitality. When the sun goddess was troubled by pernicious behaviors in prehistoric times, she shut herself up in a cave to avoid seeing evil. No one envisioned a similar withdrawal by today's leaders. A more likely model lay in the seventh century's Suiko and Shōtoku Taishi, who, when faced by challenges, sought wisdom abroad and wrote a constitution urging officials to "attend the court early in the morning, and retire late" because "the whole day is hardly enough."[32]

Chronology

660 BCE
Mythological first emperor Jimmu establishes control of Japan

200 BCE–250 CE
Yoshinogari thrives, as first known regional center

183–248 CE
Reputed dates for reign of Himiko

400–500
Height of *kofun* (mounded tomb) culture

552
Buddhism arrives in Japan, according to traditional dates

607
Suiko and Shōtoku Taishi send embassy to China

710–784
Nara serves as first "permanent" capital

752
Dedication of Great Buddha draws representatives from across Asia

794–1185
Heian serves as capital, under rule of aristocratic classes

805–806
Indigenous Buddhist sects, Tendai and Shingon, founded

894
Japan terminates embassies to China

1006–1008
Tale of Genji produced by Murasaki Shikibu

1185–1333
Kamakura serves as military capital; imperial court still in Heian

1191
Eisai of Rinzai sect establishes first Zen temple

1274, 1281
Mongol fleets attack Japan; their defeat gives rise to idea of *kamikaze*

1333–1573
Muromachi area of Kyoto serves as capital under shogun

1467–1477
Ōnin Upheaval ends Kyoto's power, initiates warring states period

1499
Rock Garden of Ryōanji in Kyoto completed

1543
Portuguese ship stranded on Tanegashima Island: first Westerners in Japan

1590
Toyotomi Hideyoshi completes military unification of Japan; two years later he unsuccessfully invades Korea

1600–1868
Edo serves as administrative capital under Tokugawa; emperors reside in Kyoto

1641
The Dutch, the only Westerners still in Japan, are restricted by Tokugawa to Dejima island, Chinese to quarters in Nagasaki

1673
Mitsui dry-goods store founded in Kyoto, the beginning of a financial giant

1688–1704
Genroku era produces a flowering of urban culture

1805
World's first use of anesthesia in surgery, by Hanaoka Seishō

1853
U.S. commodore Matthew Perry demands that Japan open its ports to American ships; his demands are granted the next year

1868
Meiji Restoration topples shogunate, initiates massive reforms

1871
Yokohama Mainichi Shimbun launched as Japan's first daily newspaper

1889
Meiji Constitution makes Japan Asia's first constitutional monarchy

1894–1895
Sino-Japanese War, won decisively by Japan; Taiwan becomes Japan's first colony

1904–1905
Russo-Japanese War, won by Japan, though not decisively

1910
Japan annexes Korea, greatly expanding its empire

1923
Great Kantō Earthquake claims nearly 140,000 lives

1925
Peace Preservation Law restricts speech; Universal Male Suffrage Law expands electorate

1931
Railway bombing in Manchuria launches Japan's takeover of northeast China and creation of Manchukuo

1937
Skirmish at Marco Polo Bridge, near Beijing, initiates Japan's second war with China

1941
World War II in Pacific begins with Japanese attack on Pearl Harbor

1945
U.S. drops atom bombs on Hiroshima and Nagasaki; Japan surrenders

1945–1952
Japan is occupied by American-led SCAP administration

1964
Summer Olympics held in Tokyo

1968
Kawabata Yasunari is first Japanese to win Nobel Prize in literature

1972
Okinawa reverts to Japanese control

1973
World oil crisis triggers inflation, new energy policies

1989
Shōwa emperor (Hirohito) dies after sixty-two years on throne

1990–1992
Bubble economy bursts, leading to a decade of economic woes

1995
Diet expresses "deep remorse" for colonialism and World War II

2003
Diet votes to send troops to Iraq, the first assignment of Self Defense Forces to an active combat zone

2009
Democratic Party of Japan ends LDP's decades-long hold on power

Notes

PREFACE

1. Edward Hallett Carr, *What Is History?* (New York: Vintage, 1961), 9.
2. Shusaku Endo, *Silence* (New York: Taplinger, 1980), xv.
3. David J. Lu, *Japan: A Documentary History* (Armonk, N.Y.: M. E. Sharpe, 1997), 352–53.
4. Edwin O. Reischauer and Albert M. Craig, *Japan: Tradition and Transformation* (Boston: Houghton Mifflin, 1978), 112.
5. Irokawa Daikichi, *The Culture of the Meiji Period* (Princeton, N.J.: Princeton University Press, 1985), 230.

CHAPTER 1

1. *Kojiki*, trans. Donald L. Philippi (Tokyo: University of Tokyo Press, 1968), 81.
2. *Niroku Shinpō*, April 14, 1900, 1.
3. *Kojiki*, 257–58.
4. *Kojiki*, 68–69.
5. See Mark J. Hudson, "Japanese Beginnings," in William M. Tsutsui, ed., *A Companion to Japanese History* (Oxford: Blackwell, 2007), 17.
6. *Nihongi: Chronicles of Japan from the Earliest Times to A.D. 697*, trans. W. G. Aston (Rutland, Vt.: Tuttle, 1972), 1:130.
7. Ibid., 1:33.
8. L. Carrington Goodrich, ed., *Japan in the Chinese Dynastic Histories: Later Han through Ming Dynasties,* trans. Ryusaku Tsunoda (South Pasadena, Calif.: P. D. and Ione Perkins, 1951), 11.
9. This and the following quotations come from *History of the Kingdom of Wei*, in Goodrich, ed., *Japan in the Chinese Dynastic Histories*, 8–16.
10. Himiko is also known as Pimiko.
11. See Conrad Totman, *A History of Japan* (Oxford: Blackwell, 2000), 48.
12. *Nihongi*, 1:110–11.
13. Ibid., 1:278–79.
14. Ibid., 1:340.
15. Ibid., 2:144, 148.
16. "New History of the T'ang Dynasty," in Ryusaku Tsunoda, Wm. Theodore De Bary, and Donald Keene, eds., *Sources of Japanese Tradition* (New York: Columbia University Press, 1958), 1:10; the Sui retort is in Delmer M. Brown, ed., *The Cambridge History of Japan,* vol. 1, *Ancient Japan* (Cambridge: Cambridge University Press, 1993), 182.
17. References to the seventeen-article "constitution" come from "Seventeen-Article Constitution of Prince Shōtoku," in Tsunoda et al., 1:48–51.
18. *History of the Sui Dynasty: The Eastern Barbarians*, in Goodrich, *Japan in the Chinese Dynastic Histories*, 29–31.
19. Joan R. Piggott, *The Emergence of Japanese Kingship* (Stanford, Calif.: Stanford University Press, 1997), 112.

20. The first use of the word *tennō*, commonly translated "emperor," was not until the late seventh century; hence my use of "king" and "queen" here for the Yamato rulers.

CHAPTER 2

1. Contribution figures from Tōdaiji records in Joan R. Piggott, *The Emergence of Japanese Kingship* (Stanford, Calif.: Stanford University Press, 1997), 267.
2. Hara Hidesaburō, "Suruga and Tōtōmi in the Kofun Age," in Joan R. Piggott, ed., *Capital and Countryside in Japan, 300–1180* (Ithaca, N.Y.: Cornell University East Asia Program, 2006), 88.
3. *Nihon shoki*, quoted in Delmer Brown, ed., *The Cambridge History of Japan,* vol. 1, *Ancient Japan* (Cambridge: Cambridge University Press, 1993), 207.
4. "Proclamation of the Emperor Shōmu," in Ryusaku Tsunoda, Wm. Theodore De Bary, and Donald Keene, eds., *Sources of Japanese Tradition* (New York: Columbia University Press, 1958), 1:104.
5. William Wayne Farris, *Population, Disease, and Land in Early Japan, 645–900* (Cambridge, Mass.: Harvard-Yenching Institute, 1985), 66.
6. "The Law of Households," in David J. Lu, *Japan: A Documentary History* (Armonk, N.Y.: M. E. Sharpe, 1997), 32.
7. *The Manyōshū*, trans. Nippon Gakujutsu Shinkōkai (New York: Columbia University Press, 1965), 206.
8. Yōrō Code: "The Law of Households," in Lu, 30; court official: *Shoku nihongi*, in Hotate Michihisa, "Traffic between Capital and Countryside in *Ritsuryō Japan,*" in Piggott, *Capital and Countryside*, 174–75.
9. K. Asakawa, *The Early Institutional Life of Japan: A Study in the Reform of 645 A.D.* (New York: Paragon Book Reprint, 1963), 337.
10. Torao Toshiba, "Nara Economic and Social Conditions," in Brown, *Cambridge History*, 423.
11. Ibid., 404.
12. Kadokawa Shoten, ed., *Man'yōshū: begināsu kurashikkusu* (Man'yōshū: Beginners' classics), bk. 4, no. 603 (Tokyo: Kadokawa Bunkō, 2001), 137.
13. Mimi Hall Yiengpruksawan, *Hiraizumi: Buddhist Art and Regional Politics in Twelfth-century Japan* (Cambridge, Mass.: Harvard University Asia Center, 1998), 27.
14. Koyama Yasunori, "East and West in the Late Classical Age," in Piggott, *Capital and Countryside*, 371.
15. Robert Borgen, *Sugawara no Michizane and the Early Heian Court* (Cambridge, Mass.: Council on East Asian Studies, Harvard University, 1986), 298.
16. Fukutō Sanae, "From Female Sovereign to Mother of the Nation: Women and Government in the Heian Period," in Mikael Adolphson et al., eds., *Heian Japan: Centers and Peripheries* (Honolulu: University of Hawai'i Press, 2007), 30.
17. Toda Yoshimi, "Kyoto and the Estate System in the Heian Period," in Piggott, *Capital and Countryside*, 249–50.
18. Charlotte Von Verschuer, "Life of Commoners in the Provinces: The *Owari no gebumi* of 988," in Adolphson et al., *Heian Japan*, 314.
19. Ivan Morris, *The World of the Shining Prince* (New York: Kodansha International, 1994), 59–60.
20. Sei Shōnagon, *The Pillow Book of Sei Shōnagon* (Baltimore: Penguin, 1971), 45, 47.
21. In Donald Keene, *Japanese Literature: An Introduction for Western Readers* (New York: Grove, 1955), 22.

22. Sei, *Pillow Book*, 210, 201, 170.

23. *Kokin wakashū* (Collection of Japanese poetry, old and new), no. 1030 (Tokyo: Iwanami Shoten, 1981), 244.

CHAPTER 3

1. *Genji and Heike: Selections from the Tale of Genji and The Tale of the Heike*, trans. Helen Craig McCullough (Stanford, Calif.: Stanford University Press, 1994), 395–96.

2. Kamo no Chōmei, "An Account of My Hut," in Donald Keene, ed., *Anthology of Japanese Literature, from the Earliest Era to the Mid-nineteenth Century* (New York: Grove Press, 1955), 200.

3. *Tales of the Heike*, in *The Ten Foot Square Hut and Tales of the Heike*, trans. A. L. Sadler (Rutland, Vt.: Tuttle, 1972), 217.

4. *The Confessions of Lady Nijō*, trans. Karen Brazell (Garden City, N.Y.: Anchor Books, 1973), 195.

5. *Gukanshō*, in Delmer Brown and Ichirō Ishida, *The Future and the Past: A Translation and Study of the Gukanshō* (Berkeley: University of California Press, 1979), 182.

6. Kozo Yamamura, ed., *The Cambridge History of Japan,* vol. 3, *Medieval Japan* (Cambridge: Cambridge University Press, 1990), 132.

7. Kadenokōji Kanenaka, diary entry, November 6, 1274, in *In Little Need of Divine Intervention: Takezaki Suenaga's Scrolls of the Mongol Invasions of Japan,* trans. and ed. Thomas Conlan (Ithaca, N.Y.: Cornell East Asia Series, 2001), 266.

8. Quoted in G. B. Sansom, *Japan: A Short Cultural History* (New York: Appleton-Century-Crofts, 1962), 323.

9. Pierre Francois Souyri, *The World Turned Upside Down: Medieval Japanese Society* (New York: Columbia University Press, 2001), 114.

10. Letters compiled by Zuikei Shōhō, in Charlotte Von Verschuer, "Ashikaga Yoshimitsu's Foreign Policy 1398 to 1408 A.D.," *Monumenta Nipponica* 62, no. 3 (autumn 2007), 280–84.

11. Donald Keene, *Yoshimasa and the Silver Pavilion* (New York: Columbia University Press, 2003), 51–52.

12. *Chronicle of Ōnin*, quoted in Mary Elizabeth Berry, *The Culture Of Civil War In Kyoto* (Berkeley: University of California Press, 1994), 29.

13. Souyri, *World Turned Upside Down*, 187.

14. Nagahara Keiji, "The Medieval Peasant," in Yamamura, *Cambridge History of Japan,* 3:333.

15. Barbara Ruch, "The Other Side of Culture in Medieval Japan," in ibid., 3:506.

16. *The Journal of Sōchō*, trans. H. Mack Horton (Stanford, Calif.: Stanford University Press, 2002), 84.

17. Souyri, *World Turned Upside Down*, 152.

18. In letters compiled by Zuikei Shōhō, 292.

19. "Tannishō," in David J. Lu, ed., *Sources of Japanese History* (New York: McGraw-Hill, 1974), 1:131.

20. Laurel Rasplica Rodd, *Nichiren: Selected Writings* (Honolulu: University of Hawai'i Press, 1980), 15, 18.

21. Ryusaku Tsunoda, Wm. Theodore De Bary, and Donald Keene, eds., *Sources of Japanese Tradition* (New York: Columbia University Press, 1958), 1:246.

22. *Tales of the Heike*, 22.

23. Kamo no Chōmei, "An Account of My Hut," 210, 211.

24. Seami Motokiyo, "Atsumori," in Keene, *Anthology*, 287, 293.

CHAPTER 4

1. Genpaku Sugita, *Dawn of Western Science in Japan: Rangaku Kotohajime* (Tokyo: Hokuseido Press, 1969), 29, 30.
2. Conrad Totman, *A History of Japan* (Malden, Mass.: Blackwell, 2000), 211.
3. Xavier letter, November 5, 1459, in C. R. Boxer, *The Christian Century in Japan 1549–1650* (Berkeley: University of California Press, 1967), 401.
4. *Master Sorai's Responsals*, trans. Samuel Yamashita (Honolulu: University of Hawai'i Press, 1994), 64, 79.
5. David John Lu, *Sources of Japanese History* (New York: McGraw-Hill, 1974), 1:216; similar orders were issued throughout the 1630s.
6. Englebert Kaempfer, *Kaempfer's Japan: Tokugawa Culture Observed* (Honolulu: University of Hawai'i Press, 1999), 191.
7. Ibid., 271.
8. Traveler Tachibana Nankei, quoted in Marcia Yonemoto, *Mapping Early Modern Japan: Space, Place, and Culture in the Tokugawa Period* (Berkeley: University of California Press, 2003), 94.
9. Mark Ravina, *Land and Lordship in Early Modern Japan* (Stanford, Calif.: Stanford University Press, 1999), 31.
10. 1643 *bakufu* regulations, in Lu, *Sources of Japanese History*, 1:209.
11. Patricia G. Sippel, "Exploiting Natural Resources in Japan's Early Modern Era: A Regional View," in Martin Collcutt et al., eds., *Japan and Its Worlds: Marius B. Jansen and the Internationalization of Japanese Studies* (Tokyo: I-House Press, 2007), 132.
12. David L. Howell, *Geographies of Identity in Nineteenth-century Japan* (Berkeley: University of California Press, 2005), 50.
13. Thomas C. Smith, *The Agrarian Origins of Modern Japan* (Stanford, Calif.: Stanford University Press, 1959), 176.
14. Anne Walthall, *Japan: A Cultural, Social, and Political History* (Boston: Houghton Mifflin, 2006), 102.
15. Katsu Kokichi, *Musui's Story: The Autobiography of a Tokugawa Samurai* (Tucson: University of Arizona Press, 1988), 60.
16. Richard Rubinger, *Popular Literacy in Early Modern Japan* (Honolulu: University of Hawai'i Press, 2007), 117.
17. Hiraga Gennai recollection, quoted in Yonemoto, *Mapping Early Modern Japan*, 118.
18. Ihara Saikaku, *The Eternal Storehouse of Japan*, in Donald Keene, ed., *Anthology of Japanese Literature: From the Earliest Era to the Mid-nineteenth Century* (New York: Grove, 1955), 361–62.
19. Trans. and evaluation of Bashō in W. G. Aston, *A History of Japanese Literature* (Rutland, Vt.: Tuttle, 1972), 292–93.
20. Anne Walthall, *Social Protest and Popular Culture in Eighteenth-century Japan* (Tucson: University of Arizona Press, 1986), 207.
21. Bob Tadashi Wakabayashi, *Anti-foreignism and Western Learning in Early-modern Japan: The New Theses of 1825* (Cambridge, Mass.: Council on East Asian Studies, Harvard University, 1986), 60.
22. *Daimyō* Tokugawa Nariaki, quoted in H. D. Harootunian, "Late Tokugawa Culture and Thought," in Marius B. Jansen, ed., *The Cambridge History of Japan*, vol. 5, *The Nineteenth Century* (Cambridge: Cambridge University Press, 1989), 190.
23. Fukuchi Gen'ichirō, *Kaiō jidan* (Recollections), in Yanagida Izumi, ed., *Fukuchi Ōchi shū* (Tokyo: Nihon Rekishi Gakkai, 1965), 298.
24. Wakabayashi, *Anti-foreignism and Western Learning*, 149.

CHAPTER 5

1. Matsubara Iwagorō, *Saiankoku no Tōkyō* (Darkest Tokyo) (Tokyo: Shūeisha, 1893; reprint, Iwanami Shoten, 1988), 130–32.

2. Francis L. Hawks, comp., *Narrative of the Expedition of an American Squadron to the China Seas and Japan* (London: MacDonald, 1952), 194.

3. Edward H. House, *The Kagoshima Affair: A Chapter of Japanese History* (Tokyo: n.p., 1875), 35.

4. Stephen Vlastos, *Peasant Protests and Uprisings in Tokugawa Japan* (Berkeley: University of California Press, 1986), 139–40.

5. Masao Maruyama, *Studies in the Intellectual History of Tokugawa Japan* (Princeton, N.J.: Princeton University Press, 1974), 362.

6. Albert M. Craig, *Chōshū in the Meiji Restoration* (Cambridge, Mass.: Harvard University Press, 1961), 336.

7. Walter W. McLaren, "Japanese Government Documents," *Transactions of the Asiatic Society of Japan* 42, pt. 1 (1914), 2.

8. Robert M. Spaulding, Jr., "The Intent of the Charter Oath," in Richard K. Beardsley, ed., *Studies in Japanese History and Politics* (Ann Arbor: University of Michigan Press, 1967), 6–7.

9. Roger Hackett, *Yamagata Aritomo in the Rise of Modern Japan, 1838–1922* (Cambridge, Mass.: Harvard University Press, 1971), 81.

10. Peter Duus, *Japanese Discovery of America* (Boston: Bedford Books, 1997), 175, 176, 182, 183.

11. Basil Hall Chamberlain, *Japanese Things, Being Notes on Various Subjects Connected with Japan* (1905; reprint, Tokyo: Tuttle, 1971), 1.

12. *The Diary of Kido Takayoshi I: 1868–1871*, trans. Sidney Devere Brown and Akiko Hirota (Tokyo: University of Tokyo Press, 1983), 190.

13. Wm. Theodore De Bary, Carol Gluck, and Arthur E. Tiedemann, comps., *Sources of Japanese Tradition*, vol. 2, pt. 2 (New York: Columbia University Press, 2006), 54.

14. James L. Huffman, *Politics of the Meiji Press: The Life of Fukuchi Gen'ichirō* (Honolulu: University of Hawai'i Press, 1980), 96.

15. *Shinano Mainichi Shimbun*, February 8, 1889, in Carol Gluck, *Japan's Modern Myths: Ideology in the Late Meiji Period* (Princeton, N.J.: Princeton University Press, 1985), 49.

16. Etsu Inagaki Sugimoto, *A Daughter of the Samurai* (Rutland, Vt.: Tuttle, 1966), 27, 62.

17. Sharon Sievers, *Flowers in Salt: The Beginnings of Feminist Consciousness in Modern Japan* (Stanford, Calif.: Stanford University Press, 1983), 55.

18. Nagatsuka Takashi, *The Soil* (Berkeley: University of California Press, 1993), 48.

19. Suzuki Hiroyuki, *Toshi e* (Toward cities), vol. 10 of *Nihon no kindai* (Japan's modern era), (Tokyo: Chūō Kōronsha, 1999), 327.

20. Steven J. Ericson, *The Sound of the Whistle: Railroads and the State in Meiji Japan* (Cambridge, Mass.: Harvard East Asian Monographs, 1996), 9.

21. Andrew Gordon, *A Modern History of Japan: From Tokugawa Times to the Present* (New York: Oxford University Press, 2003), 99–100.

22. Joseph Pittau, "Inoue Kowashi, 1843–1895, and the Foundation of Modern Japan," *Monumenta Nipponica* 20, no. 3/4 (1965), 273.

23. Uemura Masahisa, quoted in Kenneth B. Pyle, *The New Generation in Meiji Japan: Problems of Cultural Identity, 1885–1895* (Stanford, Calif.: Stanford University Press, 1969), 78.

24. The Kobe decision was reversed after a public outcry; the captain received a three-month sentence.

25. *Ōsaka Asahi Shimbun*, June 6, 1894, in Yamamoto Fumio, *Nihon shimbun hattatsu shi* (Evolution of the Japanese press) (Tokyo: Itō Shoten, 1944), 165.

26. Tsurumi Shunsuke, *Gendai Nihon shisō taikei 12: Jiyānarizumu no shisō* (Outline of modern Japanese thought 12: Philosophy of the press) (Tokyo: Chikuma Shobō, 1965), 91.

27. Miyake Setsurei editorial, *Nihon*, May 15, 1895.

28. Nimura Kazuo, *The Ashio Riot of 1907: A Social History of Mining in Japan* (Durham, N.C.: Duke University Press, 1997), 102.

29. "Wind," in Aoyagi Junrō, ed., *Meiji kyūjūkyūnen: Sesō jiken* (Ninety-nine years of Meiji: Times and events) (Tokyo: Orionsha, 1935), 121; "subhuman": Eiji Yutani, " 'Nihon no Kaso Shakai' of Gennosuke Yokoyama" (Ph.D. diss., University of California, Berkeley, 1985), 185.

30. *Kokumin Shimbun* editorial, trans. in *Japan Weekly Mail*, October 17, 1903.

CHAPTER 6

1. *Tokyo Nichi Nichi Shimbun*, February 11, 1914.

2. Junichiro Tanizaki, "Aguri," in *Seven Japanese Tales,* trans. Howard Hibbett (New York: Berkeley, 1963), 126.

3. *Chūō Kōron*, quoted in Sally Hastings, *Neighborhood and Nation in Tokyo, 1905–1937* (Pittsburgh: University of Pittsburgh Press, 1995), 127.

4. Barbara Hamill Sato, "An Alternate Informant: Middle-class Women and Mass Magazines in 1920s Japan," in Elise K. Tipton and John Clark, eds., *Being Modern in Japan: Culture and Society from the 1910s to the 1930s* (Honolulu: University of Hawai'i Press, 2000), 148.

5. Donald Keene, *Dawn to the West: Japanese Literature in the Modern Era: Fiction* (New York: Holt, 1984), 546.

6. September 1911, *Seitō*, in Tanaka Hiroshi, ed., *Kindai Nihon no jiyānarisuto* (Modern Japanese journalists) (Tokyo: Ochanomizu Shobō, 1987), 667.

7. Gregory Clancey, *Earthquake Nation* (Berkeley: University of California Press, 2006), 230.

8. Andrew Gordon, *Labor and Imperial Democracy in Prewar Japan* (Berkeley: University of California Press, 1991), 96.

9. *Red Flag*, March 15, 1928, quoted in Mikiso Hane, *Reflections on the Way to the Gallows: Voices of Japanese Rebel Women* (New York: Pantheon, 1988), 194.

10. Carol Gluck, *Japan's Modern Myths: Ideology in the Late Meiji Period* (Princeton, N.J.: Princeton University Press, 1985), 234.

11. Thomas W. Burkman, *Japan and the League of Nations: Empire and World Order, 1914–1938* (Honolulu: University of Hawai'i Press, 2008), 52.

12. Yong-ho Ch'oe, Peter H. Lee, and Wm. Theodore de Bary, eds., *Sources of Korean Tradition,* vol. 2, *From the Sixteenth to the Twentieth Centuries* (New York: Columbia University Press, 2000), 337.

13. Yukio Mishima, *Runaway Horses* (Tokyo: Tuttle, 1973), 391.

14. Economist Arisawa Hiromi, quoted in Andrew Gordon, *A Modern History of Japan from Tokugawa Times to the Present* (New York: Oxford University Press, 2003), 192.

15. *Tazan no ishi* (Stones from a different mountain) 2, no. 10 (1935), quoted in Ōta Masao, *Kiryū Yūyū* (Tokyo: Kinokuniya, 1972), 171–72.

16. Early member's statement, quoted in Richard Storry, *The Double Patriots: A Study of Japanese Nationalism* (Westport, Conn.: Greenwood, 1973), 35.

17. James L. McClain, *Japan: A Modern History* (New York: Norton, 2002), 414.

18. Saburo Shiroyama, *War Criminal: The Life and Death of Hirota Koki* (Tokyo: Kodansha International, 1977), 149.

19. Edward Behr, *Hirohito: Behind the Myth* (New York: Vintage, 1989), 138, 139.

20. Ienaga Saburō, *Japan's Past, Japan's Future: One Historian's Odyssey* (Lanham, Md.: Rowman & Littlefield, 2001), 84, 81.

21. Stephen S. Large, *Emperor Hirohito and Shōwa Japan* (London: Routledge, 1992), 53.

22. Mark Peattie, *Ishiwara Kanji and Japan's Confrontation with the West* (Princeton, N.J.: Princeton University Press, 1975), 301.

23. Haruko Taya Cook and Theodore F. Cook, *Japan at War: An Oral History* (New York: New Press, 1992), 164.

24. Gregory J. Kasza, *The State and Mass Media in Japan, 1918–1945* (Berkeley: University of California Press, 1988), 197.

25. Nobutaka Ike, ed., *Japan's Decision for War: Records of the 1941 Policy Conferences* (Stanford, Calif.: Stanford University Press, 1967), 284.

26. *Communiques Issued by the Imperial General Headquarters (Since the Outbreak of the Greater East Asian War)* (Tokyo: Mainichi, 1943), front matter.

27. Patrick Hurley, quoted in Ronald H. Spector, *Eagle against the Sun: The American War with Japan* (New York: Vintage, 1985), 115.

28. Yoshizawa Hisako, diary entry, January 22, 1945, in Samuel Hideo Yamashita, *Leaves from an Autumn of Emergencies: Selections from the Wartime Diaries of Ordinary Japanese* (Honolulu: University of Hawai'i Press, 2005), 196.

29. In Yamashita, *Leaves from an Autumn of Emergencies*, 121–22.

30. Shin Bok Su, quoted in Cook and Cook, *Japan at War*, 390.

31. Robert J. C. Butow, *Japan's Decision to Surrender* (Stanford, Calif.: Stanford University Press, 1954), 248.

CHAPTER 7

1. "Brundage Praises Role of Japanese," *Japan Times*, October 25, 1964.

2. *The Scars of War: Tokyo during World War II; Writings of Takeyama Michio*, trans. and ed. Richard H. Minear (Lanham, Md.: Rowman & Littlefield, 2007), 48.

3. Cartoon caption by Katō Etsurō, in John W. Dower, *Embracing Defeat: Japan in the Wake of World War II* (New York: Norton, 1999), 67.

4. Constitutional items from Hugh Borton, *Japan's Modern Century* (New York: Ronald Press, 1955), 493.

5. Courtney Whitney, chief of SCAP's government section, quoted in Dower, *Embracing Defeat*, 362.

6. Tetsuya Kataoka, *The Price of a Constitution: The Origin of Japan's Postwar Politics* (New York: Crane Russak, 1991), 37.

7. Dower, *Embracing Defeat*, 269.

8. Ibid., 97.

9. Masataka Kosaka, *100 Million Japanese: The Postwar Experience* (Tokyo: Kodansha, 1972), 107.

10. Journal Shufu *no tomo* (Housewife's Companion), May 1959, in Jan Bardsley, "Fashioning the People's Princess: Women's Magazines, Shōda Michiko, and the Royal Wedding of 1959," *U.S.-Japan Women's Journal*, English supp. 23 (2002), 70.

11. Journal *Shūkan Asahi* (Asahi Weekly), June 19, 1960, quoted in Hiroko Hirakawa, "Maiden Martyr for 'New Japan': The 1960 Ampo and the Rhetoric of the Other Michiko," *U.S.-Japan Women's Journal*, English supp. 23 (2002), 103.

12. Kosaka, *100 Million Japanese*, 143.

13. Kobo Abe, *The Woman in the Dunes*, trans. E. Dale Saunders (New York: Vintage, 1964), 94.

14. Neill H. McFarland, *The Rush Hour of the Gods: A Study of New Religion Movements in Japan* (New York: Macmillan, 1967).

15. Ronald P. Dore, *Shinohata: A Portrait of a Japanese Village* (New York: Pantheon, 1978), 78.

16. Frank Baldwin, "Japanese Life-Styles: The Idioms of Contemporary Japan 9: *Junpō tōsō*," *Japan Interpreter* 9, no. 2 (summer-autumn 1974), 233.

17. Timothy S. George, *Minamata: Pollution and the Struggle for Democracy in Postwar Japan* (Cambridge, Mass.: Harvard University Asia Center, 2001), 6.

18. Miyazaki Yoshikazu, "A New Price Revolution," *Japan Interpreter* 9, no. 4 (spring 1975), 449.

19. Ezra F. Vogel, *Japan as No. 1: Lessons for America* (Cambridge, Mass.: Harvard University Press, 1979), 8.

20. Arai Shinya, *Shoshaman: A Tale of Corporate Japan*, trans. Chieko Mulhern (Berkeley: University of California Press, 1991), 221.

21. John Mock, "Mother or Mama: The Political Economy of Bar Hostesses in Sapporo," in Anne E. Imamura, ed., *Re-imaging Japanese Women* (Berkeley: University of California Press, 1996), 185.

22. *Springfield (Ohio) News-Sun*, July 27, 1980, 7A. A few years later, the advertiser became a Toyota dealer.

23. John W. Dower, *War without Mercy: Race and Power in the Pacific War* (New York: Pantheon, 1986), 315.

24. Narai Osamu, "The Ceiling over Japan's Economy," *Japan Echo* 26, no. 5 (October 1999), 44.

25. Sassa Atsuyuki, "Fault Lines in Our Emergency Management System," *Japan Echo* 22, no. 2 (summer 1995), 24.

26. Jeffrey Kingston, *Japan in Transformation: 1952–2000* (Harlow, England: Longman, 2001), 141.

27. "Japan Faces Economic Headache from Ageing Population," Reuters, September 12, 2007, www.reuters.com/article/idUST20992820070912.

28. John Nathan, *Japan Unbound: A Volatile Nation's Quest for Pride and Purpose* (Boston: Houghton Mifflin, 2004), 115.

29. "Nomo's Heroics and Japan-U.S. Relations," *Shokun* (Ladies and Gentlemen!), September 1995, trans. in *Japan Echo* 22, no. 4 (winter 1995), 80.

30. Kenzaburo Oe, *A Healing Family*, trans. Stephen Snyder (Tokyo: Kodansha International, 1995), 95.

31. Nathan, *Japan Unbound*, 109.

32. Ryusaku Tsunoda, Wm. Theodore De Bary, and Donald Keene, eds., *Sources of Japanese Tradition* (New York: Columbia University Press, 1958), 1:49–50.

Further Reading

GENERAL SURVEYS AND DOCUMENT COLLECTIONS

De Bary, Wm. Theodore, Carol Gluck, and Arthur E. Tiedemann, eds. *Sources of Japanese Tradition*. 2nd ed. 2 vols. New York: Columbia University Press, 2001–2006.

Keene, Donald, ed. *Anthology of Japanese Literature: From the Earliest Era to the Mid–nineteenth Century*. New York: Grove Press, 1955.

———. *Modern Japanese Literature*. New York: Grove Press, 1956.

Lu, David J. *Japan: A Documentary History*. Armonk, N.Y.: M. E. Sharpe, 1997.

Minear, Richard, ed. *Through Japanese Eyes*. 4th ed. New York: Apex Press, 2008.

Morris, Ivan. *The Nobility of Failure: Tragic Heroes in the History of Japan*. New York: Holt, Rinehart and Winston, 1975.

Mulhern, Chieko Irie, ed. *Heroic with Grace: Legendary Women of Japan*. Armonk, N.Y.: M. E. Sharpe, 1991.

Sansom, George. *Japan: A Short Cultural History*. New York: Appleton Century Crofts, 1962.

Totman, Conrad. *A History of Japan*. Malden, Mass.: Blackwell, 2000.

Varley, H. Paul. *Japanese Culture*. 4th ed. Honolulu: University of Hawai'i Press, 2000.

Walthall, Anne. *Japan: A Cultural, Social, and Political History*. Boston: Houghton Mifflin, 2006.

EARLY AND CLASSICAL JAPAN (TO 1160)

Adolphson, Mikael, Edward Kamens, and Stacie Matsumoto, eds. *Heian Japan: Centers and Peripheries*. Honolulu: University of Hawai'i Press, 2007.

Barnes, Gina L. *State Formation in Japan: Emergence of a 4th-Century Ruling Elite*. London: Routledge, 2007.

Morris, Ivan. *The World of the Shining Prince: Court Life in Ancient Japan*. New York: Kodansha America, 1994.

Murasaki Shikibu. *The Tale of Genji*. Trans. Edwin Seidensticker. New York: Knopf, 1978.

———. Trans. Royall Tyler. New York: Penguin, 2001.

———. Trans. Arthur Waley. New York: Modern Library, 1960.

Piggott, Joan R. *The Emergence of Japanese Kingship*. Stanford, Calif.: Stanford University Press, 1997.

MEDIEVAL AND EARLY MODERN JAPAN (1160–1850)

Berry, Mary Elizabeth. *The Culture of Civil War in Kyoto*. Berkeley: University of California Press, 1994.

Cooper, Michael, ed. *They Came to Japan: An Anthology of European Reports on Japan, 1543–1640*. Berkeley: University of California Press, 1965.

Friday, Karl. *Samurai, Warfare and the State in Early Medieval Japan*. New York: Routledge, 2004.

Kaempfer, Englebert. *Kaempfer's Japan: Tokugawa Culture Observed*. Honolulu: University of Hawai'i Press, 1999.

Katsu Kokichi. *Musui's Story: The Autobiography of a Tokugawa Samurai.* Tucson: University of Arizona Press, 1988.

Keene, Donald. *Yoshimasa and the Silver Pavilion: The Creation of the Soul of Japan.* New York: Columbia University Press, 2003.

Mass, Jeffrey P., ed. *The Origins of Japan's Medieval World.* Stanford, Calif.: Stanford University Press, 1997.

Matsuo Bashō. *The Narrow Road to the North and Other Travel Sketches.* Trans. Nobuaki Yuasa. New York: Penguin, 1966.

Souyri, Pierre François. *The World Turned Upside Down: Medieval Japanese Society.* New York: Columbia University Press, 2001.

The Ten Foot Square Hut and Tales of the Heike. Trans. A. L. Sadler. Rutland, Vt.: Tuttle, 1972.

MODERN JAPAN: SURVEYS

Allinson, Gary D. *Japan's Postwar History.* Ithaca, N.Y.: Cornell University Press, 1997.

Gordon, Andrew. *A Modern History of Japan from Tokugawa Times to the Present.* 2nd ed. New York: Oxford University Press, 2009.

Hane, Mikiso. *Peasants, Rebels, Women, and Outcastes: The Underside of Modern Japan.* Lanham, Md.: Rowman & Littlefield, 2003.

Huffman, James L. *Modern Japan: A History in Documents.* New York: Oxford University Press, 2004.

McClain, James L. *Japan: A Modern History.* New York: Norton, 2002.

Seidensticker, Edward. *Low City, High City: Tokyo from Edo to the Earthquake.* Rutland, Vt.: Tuttle, 1983.

Walthall, Anne, ed. *Modern Japan: The Human Tradition.* Wilmington, Del.: SR Books, 2002.

MODERN JAPAN: THE NINETEENTH CENTURY

Benfey, Christopher. *The Great Wave: Gilded Age Misfits, Japanese Eccentrics, and the Opening of Old Japan.* New York: Random House, 2003.

Duus, Peter. *The Japanese Discovery of America: A Brief History with Documents.* Boston: Bedford, 1997.

Fukuzawa Yukichi. *The Autobiography of Yukichi Fukuzawa.* New York: Columbia University Press, 1966.

Irokawa Daikichi. *The Culture of the Meiji Period.* Trans. Marius B. Jansen. Princeton, N.J.: Princeton University Press, 1985.

Tsurumi, Patricia. *Factory Girls: Women in the Thread Mills of Meiji Japan.* Princeton, N.J.: Princeton University Press, 1990.

MODERN JAPAN: THE TWENTIETH CENTURY

Bix, Herbert. *Hirohito and the Making of Modern Japan.* New York: HarperCollins, 2000.

Cook, Haruko Taya, and Theodore F. Cook. *Japan at War: An Oral History.* New York: New Press, 1992.

Dower, John W. *Embracing Defeat: Japan in the Wake of World War II.* New York: New Press, 1999.

———. *War without Mercy: Race & Power in the Pacific War.* New York: Pantheon, 1986.

Field, Norma. *In the Realm of a Dying Emperor.* New York: Vintage, 1993.

Hane, Mikiso. *Reflections on the Way to the Gallows: Voices of Japanese Rebel Women.* New York: Pantheon, 1988.

Hein, Laura, and Mark Selden. *Living with the Bomb: American and Japanese Cultural Conflicts in the Nuclear Age.* Armonk, N.Y.: M. E. Sharpe, 1997.

Yamashita, Samuel Hideo. *Leaves from an Autumn of Emergencies: Selections from the Wartime Diaries of Ordinary Japanese.* Honolulu: University of Hawai'i Press, 2005.

Websites

About Japan
http://aboutjapan.japansociety.org/
Includes thirty essays on varied topics from Japanese history and society, all by recognized scholars; also includes teaching resources.

Ancient Japan
www.wsu.edu:8080/~dee/ANCJAPAN/ CONTENTS.HTM
Basic information about Japan's history, religion, and cultural life from earliest times through the twelfth century.

Asia for Educators
http://afe.easia.columbia.edu/
Designed primarily for teachers, this site contains outlines, lesson plans, source materials, and timelines that will also be useful to students.

Doing Photography and Social Research in the Allied Occupation of Japan, 1948–1951
http://library.osu.edu/sites/rarebooks/japan/ about.html
Sizeable collection of images of Japan during the immediate post–World War II years, with related textual documents.

Education about Asia
www.aasianst.org/EAA/index.htm
Site of the leading journal for teaching about Japan and Asia, with indexes to back issues, interviews with influential specialists, and links to other Asia-related materials.

Hiroshima Peace Memorial Museum
www.pcf.city.hiroshima.jp/index_e2.html
The major museum at the site of the first atomic bomb presents virtual tours, historical descriptions, and recollections, both written and spoken, from survivors.

Internet East Asian History Sourcebook
www.fordham.edu/halsall/eastasia/ eastasiasbook.html#Japan
An extensive collection of primary texts, literary works, and historical summaries, collected from many online sites, usually (but not always) citing the original sources.

Metropolitan Museum of Art, New York
www.metmuseum.org/Works_of_Art/ asian_art
Large collection of photographs of Asian paintings, sculptures, and ceramics, with detailed explanations. The museum's timeline (www.metmuseum.org/toah/) is also useful for its explanations of both history and art.

MIT: Visualizing Cultures
http://ocw.mit.edu/ans7870/21f/21f.027j/ menu/index.html
Outstanding visual materials on Westerners in Japan, Meiji life, wars, and atomic bombs, with accompanying historical essays and teaching suggestions, mostly by Pulitzer Prize–winning historian John Dower.

Museum of Fine Arts, Boston: Art of Asia, Oceana, Africa
www.mfa.org/collections/index.asp?key=21
Large collection of Japanese works of art from earliest times to the present, with special sections on arms and armor, Buddhist art, postcards, woodblock prints, and Meiji-era photographs.

National Diet Library, Japan
www.ndl.go.jp/en/index.html
Japan's leading library contains a variety of historical materials, including photographs, documents about the 1947 constitution, and letters of important figures; most holdings are available in both English and Japanese.

National Museum of Japanese History
www.rekihaku.ac.jp/english/index.html
This guide to Japan's leading historical museum provides explanations, with historical context, of special exhibits on a wide range of topics: woodblock prints, wars, ancient emperors, Japanese shrines, and many others.

Portals to the World—History: Japan
www.loc.gov/rr/international/asian/japan/
resources/japan-history.html
U.S. Library of Congress site providing links to major sources for Japanese history, many of them in Japan.

Samurai Archives
www.samurai-archives.com/
Voluminous sources of every kind of information about samurai: prints, historical essays, biographies of hundreds of warriors (including twenty-six women), and maps.

Stanford Guide to Japan Information Resources
http://jguide.stanford.edu/
Created at Stanford University, this guide provides one of the most extensive

guides to information about various areas of Japanese life, including history, photo collections, essays on controversial issues, historical comic books, museum guides, and World War II images.

Virtual Religion Index
http://virtualreligion.net/vri/
A guide to articles on different religious traditions, including Shintō, Buddhism, and Confucianism.

Welcome to Edo
www.us-japan.org/edomatsu/home.html
An impressive visual introduction to the city of Edo, now named Tokyo: maps, woodblock prints, and links to other historical materials.

Acknowledgments

All acts of writing are communal, none more so than the writing of a historical survey. Never, in anything I have written, have I felt more deeply my dependence on others. First, there are Clio's giants: people as varied as George Sansom, Anne Walthall, E. H. Norman, and James McClain, whose own syntheses have inspired and informed mine. My debt to them is huge, as it is to Bill Tsutsui, whose recent work on historiography has provided a rich overview of Japanese history as it now stands. I am also pleased to be able to thank publicly those who helped me find sources and made library collections available, particularly Suzanne Smailes at Wittenberg University, Ann Harrington and Ursula Scholz at Loyola University Chicago, and James McMahon at Northwestern University. My debt is deep to many who have given me both advice and resources, sometimes reading portions of my manuscripts, sometimes helping me think issues through, sometimes saving me from blunders. They include, in particular, Judith Ames, Dennis Frost, Sally Hastings, Nao Hoshino-Huffman, Mark Hudson, Amy Stanley, my sister Judy (whose probing questions were more helpful than she would ever admit), Jeremy Hunter, Hamura Shoei Yoh, and Bob Rafferty. I have been the beneficiary of exceptional readers and editors, too, people both incisive and kind: Anand Yang, Bonnie Smith, my copy editor Martha Ramsey, Joellyn Ausanka, who oversaw the production process, two unusually helpful anonymous readers—and Nancy Toff, who advised me continually, with a skill and care such as I have never seen before. The final thanks go to my amazing family: James, Nao, and Ryu-chan in Tokyo; Kristen, Dave, Grace, and Simon in Chicago; and my mother, June, in Indiana. They don't merely support me; they give me energy, ideas, direction, humor when I get too serious—and love. I am a debtor indeed!

Index

Bureaucracy, 71
Burma, 106
Bushi. See Samurai
Bushidō myth. 46, 60
Byōdōin, 32, 33

Cabinet, 81, 88, 91, 95, 100, 104, 105
Cabinet Policy Bureau, 104
Café culture, 92–93, 95, 100
Calendar, Western, 77, 81
Calligraphy, 32, 34, 52–53
Capitalism, 43–44, 49, 65, 84, 95
Cap rank system, 15, 17
Carr, Edward Hallett, xi
Castle towns, 64
Castles, 45, 56, 59
CBS Records, 120
Celadon, 49
Cell phones. *See* Telephone technology
Censorship, 87–88, 91, 96, 105, 112
Census, 22, 29, 58
Ceramics, xiii, 7, 50
Chang'an, 19, 21
Charter Oath, 76
Cherry-blossom viewing, 3, 44, 87
Chiang Kai-shek, 100, 103, 104
Chikamatsu Monzaemon, 67
China
    descriptions of Japan, 9–10, 16
    domestic developments, 7, 27, 41, 88, 103,
        112, 118
    influence on Japan, 13–16, 19, 21–23, 25,
        32, 51–52, 54, 61, 66
    Japanese colonialism, 85, 99–100, 103
    relations with Japan, 27–28, 44, 61, 78, 89,
        96–98, 118, 128, 129
    trade with Japan, 49–50, 57, 60–61, 99,
        127, 129
    wars with Japan, 20, 56, 85–86, 104–6, 108,
        112, 130
Chisso chemical company, 117
Chongqing, 104
Chōnin (townsmen), 65–70
Chōshū domain, 70, 75–76
Choson dynasty (Korea), 50
Christian Marxism, 95
Christianity xii, 57, 78, 80
Chūō Kōron, 124
Cities and towns, 4, 9, 48–49, 58, 61, 62,
    64–67, 129
Citizens, 87, 90, 91, 117, 118, 124
Citizens movements, 117, 118
Civilian deaths in war, 86, 104, 106–8
Civil liberties, 111
Civil war (Boshin), 73–74
Class distinctions, 9, 44, 55, 60, 72, 74, 76, 77,
    87. *See also* Status system
Climate change, 4–5, 6, 10, 12, 128

Cloistered government. See *Insei*
Clothing. *See* Attire
Coal, 84, 103
Coins, 21, 49, 50
Colonialism, 85, 96–98, 99–100, 103, 108,
    122, 130
Comfort women, 108, 124
Commerce, 30, 37, 47, 49–51, 62, 63–64.
    See also Trade
Commercial treaties, 74, 75, 85, 105
Committee on Literature, 95
Commodity futures market, 65
Commoners xii, xiii–xiv, 9, 16–17, 28, 54, 61,
    66, 67, 70, 77, 91, 95, 115
    culture, 25, 40, 93, 125
    daily life, 9, 23–24, 40, 47–48, 62–64, 72,
        87, 106, 120–21, 124–25
    religion, 24–25, 51–52, 54
Communism, 95, 102–4, 112
Compulsory education, 78–80
Confucianism, 14–16, 60, 66, 71
Constitution (Meiji), 80–81, 110, 130
Constitution (1947), 110–12, 114, 128
Consumers, 92, 115–16, 122, 125, 127
Copper, 21
Coral Sea battle, 106
Corruption, official, 31, 81, 91, 95, 101, 119,
    124, 128
Cotton, 50, 63
Council of State, 22, 23, 77
Council on Shrine Affairs, 22, 23
Court Music Bureau, 25
Craftsmen, 60, 65
Crops, 47–48, 63
Currency, 62, 83

Daibutsu, 19, 21, 25, 129
Daimyō, 43, 45–47, 49, 50, 55–62, 64, 71, 75, 77
Dairy farms, 78
Dakkochan, 115
Dancing, 25, 31, 32, 67, 78
Dannoura battle, 38–39
Dazaifu, 23, 28
Defense spending. *See* Military budgets
Dejima, 61, 129
Demilitarization, 110–12. *See also* Pacifism
Democracy, 80–81, 95, 101, 110–12, 114, 128
Democratic Party of Japan, 130
Demonstrations, 90, 91, 95, 98, 114, 115, 118
deNA internet firm, 127
Department stores, 87, 92
Diet, 80–81, 95, 101, 102, 111, 114, 117,
    124, 130
Diplomacy, 9, 10–11, 15, 17, 41, 50, 60, 73,
    89, 96, 109
Disarmament, 11, 113–14
Discrimination, 83–84, 93, 122
Divorce rates, 126

Iwakura Mission, 78
Iwakura Tomomi, 76
Iyo, 10
Izanagi, 3, 13
Izanami, 13

Japan As Number One, 119
Japan bashing, 121
Japan Nitrogen Fertilizer Company, 101
Japan–U.S. Security Treaty, 114, 115, 118
Japanese-Asian relations, xii–xii, 3, 7, 10–11,
  13–14, 18, 20, 27–28, 37, 41, 121, 124,
  129. *See also specific countries*
Jazz, 92
Jewelry, 6, 11, 93
Jien, 41
Jilin, 100
Jimmu, 13, 129
Jingoism, 86, 89–90
Jingū, 3
Jitō (emperor), 20
Jitō (estate steward), 40–41, 43, 45
Jiyū minken (freedom and people's rights)
  movement, 80–81
Joint Declaration of the Powers, 108
Jōmon period, 4–8
Jōmon pottery, 4, 5, 6
Journalism. *See* Press
Justice Ministry, 100, 105

Kabuki, 67, 68
Kaempfer, Englebert, 61
Kagoshima, 74
Kamado (clay cooking stove), 13
Kamakura (city), 38, 39, 129
Kamakura period, 38–42, 47, 49, 51–52
Kamba Michiko, 115
Kambayashi Akatsuki, 93
Kami (god-spirits), 22, 32, 47, 80
Kamikaze (divine winds), 41–42, 129
Kammu, 27
Kamo Chōmei, 52
Kamo River, 67
Kana, 28
Kanagawa, Treaty of, 73
Kanji, 4, 28
Kanno Suga, 95
Kanō school of painting, 53
Kanrei (deputy shogun), 43
Karafuto, 98
Karaoke, 128
Kasa, Lady, 25
Katsu Kokichi, 64
Kawabata Yasunari, 102, 130
Kawakami Hajime, 95
Kawaraban. *See* Broadsides
Kemmu Restoration, 42–43
Ki Tsurayuki, 34

Kido Takayoshi, 75, 80
Kikkoman. *See* Noda Shōyu
Kinai region, 13–14, 39
King magazine, 93
Kinkakuji villa, 44, 53
Kiryū Yūyū, 101
Kiyomizu temple, 26
Kobe, 74, 85, 94, 124
Kōfukuji, 29
Kofun period, 4, 11–17, 129
Kofun (tombs), 4, 11
Kōgyoku, 17
Koizumi Jun'ichirō, 126–127
Kojiki, 3, 13, 25
Kōken, 19, 21
Kokinshū, 35
Kokugaku (national learning), 66, 71
Kokumo (mother of nation), 29
Kokutai (national polity), 96
Kokutai no hongi (Cardinal principles of the
  national polity), 102
Kōmeitō, 116
Korea, 41, 50, 108
  colonialism, 96–100, 103, 124, 130
  immigrants in Japan, 93, 96
  influence on Japan, 7, 11–12, 14, 15, 19
  Japan's intrusions, 3, 13–14, 20, 56, 81, 85,
    88–89, 129
  relations with Japan, 17, 27, 49, 50, 60,
    124, 128
Korean War, 113
Kōtoku Shūsui, 95
Kōzanji, 31
Kublai Khan, 41
Kūkai, 33–34
Kumagai Naozane, 37, 52
Kume Kunitake, 78
Kuni (country), 22, 62
"*Kuni no tame*" (For the good of the country),
  76, 84
Kurosawa Akira, 128
Kūya, 33
Kwantung Army. *See* Guandong Army
Kyōgen plays, 52
Kyoto, 37, 39, 41–44, 58, 64, 67, 74, 75, 77,
  129

L. L. Bean, 125
Labor, 94, 110, 112, 119
Land tax, 80, 82–83
Landholding, 17, 22–23, 29–30, 56, 110
Law codes, premodern, 15, 20, 21, 46, 58, 62
League of Blood, 102
League of Nations, 96, 103
Legal penalties, 17, 23, 40, 47
Legends. *See* Myths
Legislature, 80–81. *See also* Diet
Leprosy, 48

The
New
Oxford
World
History

General Editors
Bonnie G. Smith
Rutgers University

Anand A. Yang
University of Washington

Editorial Board
Donna Guy
Ohio State University

Karen Ordahl Kupperman
New York University

Margaret Strobel
University of Illinois, Chicago

John O. Voll
Georgetown University

The New Oxford World History
provides a comprehensive, synthetic
treatment of the "new world history"
from chronological, thematic, and
geographical perspectives, allowing
readers to access the world's complex
history from a variety of conceptual,
narrative, and analytical viewpoints
as it fits their interests.

James L. Huffman is H. Orth Hirt
Professor of History Emeritus at
Wittenberg University. A newspaper
reporter in his early years, he also
taught at Dartmouth College, the
University of Nebraska–Lincoln, and
Indiana Wesleyan University. He is the
author or editor of five other books
on Japan, including *Modern Japan:
A History in Documents* (2004),
*Creating a Public: People and Press in
Meiji Japan* (1997), and *A Yankee in
Meiji Japan: The Crusading Journalist
Edward H. House* (2003). He lives in
Chicago, where he is studying the daily
lives of commoners in Japan's early
twentieth century.

The
New
Oxford
World
History

CHRONOLOGICAL VOLUMES
The World from 4000 to 1000 BCE
The World from 1000 BCE to 300/500 CE
The World from 300 to 1000 CE
The World from 1000 to 1500
The World from 1450 to 1700
The World in the Eighteenth Century
The World in the Nineteenth Century
The World in the Twentieth Century

THEMATIC AND TOPICAL VOLUMES
The City: A World History
Democracy: A World History
Empires: A World History
The Family: A World History
Race: A World History
Technology: A World History

GEOGRAPHICAL VOLUMES
Central Asia in World History
China in World History
Japan in World History
Russia in World History
The Silk Road in World History
South Africa in World History
South Asia in World History
Southeast Asia in World History
Trans-Saharan Africa in World History